Indian Ringneck

Indian Ringnecks as pets
Indian Ringneck Keeping, Pros and Cons, Care, Housing, Diet and Health.

by

Roger Rodendale

Table of Contents

Table of Contents 2

Introduction 3

Chapter 1: All About Indian Ringnecks 5

Chapter 2: Buying a Ringneck and Being Prepared 21

Chapter 3:Welcome Birdie 55

Chapter 4: Breeding Ringnecks 72

Chapter 5: Health Issues in Indian Ringnecks.................... 79

Conclusion... 103

References 104

Introduction

Parrots belong to a species called Psittacines. Of all the birds that have been domesticated in this species, the Indian Ringnecked parrot is one of the most elegant and most sought after ones. These birds are brightly colored in shades of green and blue. They are so popular globally that they are the first visual representation of the entire species. So when you are picturing a parrot, you are probably thinking of the Indian Ringneck.

These birds are found in the wild in parts of Asia and Africa, where they originated, but they have been domesticated for so many centuries that they are usually considered to be meant only for domestication. So, quite obviously, they make wonderful pets and will be your best companion for years to come.

Indian Ringnecks, like all parrots, are extremely intelligent and are therefore easy to train to perform several tricks. They are also easy to train to talk, which makes them extremely entertaining as well. They form strong bonds with humans and will face severe physical and mental issues when they are not taken care of properly.

Their quirky personality can be very endearing, which is why they are among the most popular options for pet parrots. This also means that they are readily available, making it easy for you to bring one home when you are ready for one.

It is not enough to leave your parrot in a cage with a bowl of birdseed. You must understand what is actually needed for their mental and physical well being. If this is your first time with a parrot, it is best that you read up as much as you can about these birds before you make a commitment to one. They live for as long as 50 years, hence it is quite a big deal to bring a parrot home.

With this book, you will get all the information you need, starting from how to identify the bird, choosing a healthy bird for your home, making sure that you form a strong bond and also keeping the parrot healthy and happy for life.

The tips that you will read about in this book are easy to apply and are highly effective. They are the result of discussions with parrot owners. So, you can be sure that the information that you find in this book is accurate and perfectly applicable to your feathered friend.

The book aims at helping not only beginners but also those who are dealing with issues with their current pets. Whether you are finding it hard to think of new ways to entertain your bird or are uncertain about the food that you are providing to him, you will certainly find ample assistance with this book.

The aim is to prepare you for your new pet and make sure that you are able to provide him or her with a home that is happy.

Chapter 1: All About Indian Ringnecks

With this chapter, we will look at the history and the physical description of the Indian Ringneck. Having this information will not only help you select the right bird for your home, but will also tell you what to expect from your Indian Ringneck.

1. Physical description

These elegant parrots are available in a range of bright and pastel colors. From green to buttercup yellow and lime green, they are beautifully feathered. The distinct ring around the neck gives them their name and they can be distinguished by their long tail.

These parrots are medium sized and usually measure between 36 and 43 cm in length. Their long tail makes for half the length of the body. The wings are up to 7 inches in length. They are also light in comparison to other parrots their size. They usually weigh between 115 and 140 grams.

The hooked beak and the long tail are the most distinguishing physical traits. The beak is usually red in color and has a black tip. In the case of the lower bill, a paler tip that is blackish in color is observed. As for the feet, they contrast with the beak and are usually greenish slate or ashy slate in color. The iris of the bird is pale yellow in color and gives the eyes a sparkle.

In the wild, their coloration is green with a hue of bluish grey or yellow. The under plumage has these hues and is lighter than the primary plumage.

The nape of the neck sometimes has a hint of blue that may go down to the back of the head. The tail feathers are bright green in color. There may be a central tail feather that has a yellowish green tinge. The chin area has a distinct black strip that runs straight down.

For most part, the male and the female look similar to one another. They are almost identical. However, you can tell a mature male apart in most cases unless there have been any color mutations. There is a black band on the red neckband that extends just above the beak and goes up to the eyes. You have another wide band that goes down from the lower bill and then becomes thinner at the sides of the parrot's neck. This line then connects with the ring on the neck before going up to the back of the neck. If there is a color mutation, mostly blue, the male parrot will have a white collar instead of a black one.

In the case of females, the black line is absent. In most cases even the ring around the neck is absent. If the female does have a ring, it is usually very pale in color.

When the birds are younger, you cannot tell them apart and it is best that you opt for techniques like DNA gender testing. You can even choose surgical methods of determining the exact gender of your bird.

Juvenile Ringnecks look just like the adult female. The plumage is slightly dull in color. They have no black markings on the chin and neck, the ring around the neck is absent and the blue tint usually seen in a mature male is not seen.

The juveniles get the same plumage as the adults when they are about 2 years old or when they are just about to turn three. However, in some rare cases, you will be able to see a faint red collar around the neck of the bird when he is barely a year old.

2. Taxonomy

The Indian Ringneck is also commonly known as the rose ringed parakeet. It is a tropical parrot that has Afro-Asian origins. It is classified under the genus name *Psittacula,* which is Latin for "parrot", derived from the word *psittacus.* The scientific name of the Indian Ringneck is *Psittaculakrameri* to commemorate an Austrian naturalist named Wilhelm Heinrich Kramer. A phylogenetic analysis of the DNA reveals that the Indian Ringneck is very closely related to the Mauritius parakeet. There have been several speculations that this bird should be classified somewhere in between the Asian and African subspecies of the Indian Ringneck Parrot.

Four subspecies of the Indian Ringneck have been identified. They are broadly classified as the African and Asian Subspecies, which are further classified as:

- The African rose ringed parakeet: This parrot is commonly found in the west African region covering Senegal, Guinea, southern Mauritania and the entire expanse from the east to west of Uganda, south Sudan and Egypt. These birds reside with other parrots in the Nile valley and also Giza. A few populations have also been seen in Sinai and the northern coast of Africa. In the 1980s, a few populations of this subspecies also began to breed in parts of Israel. In these areas, they are considered an invasive species.

- **Abyssinian rose ringed parakeet:** These birds are commonly seen in the entire western coast across the northern part of Sennar and Ethiopia including Sudan and the Northwestern part of Somalia.

- **Indian rose ringed parakeet:** This subspecies is of Asian origin and is known to have its roots in the Southern part of the Indian subcontinent. There are feral populations all over the world. Today, they are commonly seen in the United States, Britain and Australia among other western nations.

- **Boreal rose ringed parakeet:** This sub-species is normally seen in the northern part of India, Bangladesh, Burma, Pakistan and Nepal. They have also been introduced to other countries across the globe, where their feral populations have thrived quite well.

The distribution of these birds all over the world shows that they have been valued as pets for a long time. In fact, since the time of the Roman Empire, these birds have been mentioned quite frequently in literature and artwork. It is interesting to see how a tropical species of parrot has gained worldwide popularity. It is due to the personality of the bird, their temperament and their compatibility with human beings.

3. Difference between African and Asian Ringnecks

As we discussed in the previous section, there are two broad categories of the Ringnecked parrot: the Asian and the African varieties. They are very similar in appearance and it may be confusing for someone who is not very familiar with parrots to tell them apart. The common thing is that they both make great pets and you can decide to bring either one home.

The differences, although minute, are quite significant. Especially if you want to bring one home, you should know which one you are choosing. Here are the differences that will help you spot the right species:

Differences in color

- For the most part, the African Ringneck looks very similar to the Asian variety. While the Indian Ringneck has vibrant green plumes, the African variety usually has a lime green outer feathering.

- The black ring that you find around the neck of the male bird is thicker in the case of the African variety and is also a lot more prominent.

- The rose colored ring, on the other hand, is brighter and more conspicuous in the case of the Indian Ringneck.

- The beak of the Indian Ringneck is bright red in color while the African Ringneck has a beak that is plum colored.

Differences in size

- The size of the tail and the body is a significant differentiator between the two species.

- The African Ringneck is much smaller and is almost the size of a cockatiel. These birds usually measure between 11-13 inches in length.

- The Indian Ringneck on the other hand is larger and can grow up to 16 inches in size.

- The tail to body ratio is different too. In the case of the African Ringnecks, the tail is much longer than the body when compared to the Indian variety.

- They also differ in weight with the Indian variety being heavier at about 125 grams while the African Ringneck is not more than 120 grams in weight.

Difference in personality
- It is a common observation that the Indian Ringneck is more aggressive in comparison to the African variety. Therefore, the latter is normally recommended for someone with no experience with parrots.

- With Indian Ringnecks, you will have to be more patient, will have to provide more positive reinforcement and will also have to be slightly dominating.

- You will see that the Indian Ringnecks will be more nippy and noisy when they are younger.

- One common thing is that they do not really like to cuddle. With the African variety, they will tolerate being petted along the side of their neck while they perch on your shoulder. Both birds do not like to be touched on any other part of their body.

So, knowing the difference is crucial to the preparations that you make. The way you handle them and bond with them will also differ based on whether you bring home an African Ringneck or an Indian Ringneck Parrot.

4. History of Ringnecks
For several centuries, Indian Ringnecks have been domesticated and have been great companions to people. They are particularly popular in India and Pakistan and have been mentioned in folklore and ancient literature frequently.

These parrots also took the fancy of several foreigners and were exported all over the world. Legend has it that Alexander the Great developed such fondness for these birds that he had them exported around the Mediterranean Area. This is probably why their numbers increased so rapidly all over the globe.

Today they are common household pets in countries like the United Kingdom, South Africa, the United States and Australia.

These birds originated in India, parts of central and Eastern Africa and Burma. Their introduction in European countries is accredited to several monarchs and invaders who made their way into these countries and then exported the birds back home.

The ancient Greeks were quite familiar with these birds. This is evident from the records maintained by Archimedes that date back to 200BC. They have been found in Great Britain for almost two hundred years now. A few of them also belonged to the Royal Family of England.

In the 1920s, Alfred Ezra imported several birds. He was born in India and had a fascination with birds from a very young age. He successfully bred parrots to produce a mutated species called the Lutino. However, these birds were not in great health and died very early. They often died before they hatched and sometimes immediately after they left the nest.

By the year 1932, the Duke of Bedford, who had several Lutino birds on his estate, was able to produce healthy birds. After this, the species began to become more established.

It was in the year 1934 that Alfred Ezra bred the perfect Lutino birds. By then, several bird farms had also begun the practice of breeding this mutated species.

In the year 1920, a paper titled "Variations among birds" was written by Masauji Hachisuka. He mentioned two blue Indian Ringnecks in the paper that were bred in Calcutta by a man named M.G Mallick. There were several myths about these birds, such as they were both males who were kept in cages made of gold! It was also believed that these birds were never bred with other birds to breed other species.

It wasn't until after the Second World War that a blue Ringneck was produced in an aviary. It was in the aviary of a British soldier who resided in India. Two of his green Ringnecks bred to give birth to one that was blue.

By the year 1947, the number of Lutino Ringnecks were fast increasing. In fact, their numbers were almost the same as the regular Ringnecks in countries like England.

In the USA, however, not even one Lutino bird was found. In the year 1948, Sidney Porter conducted a lot of research on this variety and then obtained two green and two Lutino birds by 1949. They were bred in Fillmore, California to start the population of Lutino birds in the USA.

By now, the Indian Ringneck parrot was really a prized bird. They were sold for huge sums in India to foreigners who showed keen interest in them. There are records of two blue Ringnecks that were sold to breeders named George West and Harold Rudkin by a dealer in Calcutta for $1000 back in 1948. These two birds were believed to be the only live ones in captivity.

In order to protect these exotic birds, strict laws were made in the USA regarding the import of psittacines. One could only bring in the bird if they had kept them for at least 30 days. Then the bird qualified as a family pet and was allowed into the USA. Sadly, neither West nor Rudkin were able to gather proof that the bird had been with them for that period. So, the only two blues were returned to India.

It is believed that these birds were later obtained by the Duke of Bedford in the same year. He sent the two birds to David West in 1952 after which a successful breeding program to create blue Ringnecks came into practice.

A wealthy aviculturist named Ray Thomas then imported two turquoise birds from Calcutta. These birds were called blue Simon. Yet since their color was not the original blue, Thomas did not return the birds and neither did he pay for them. He was, no doubt, very fond of them. Upon Thomas' death, these two birds were taken in by Gordon Hayes and Dave West, who began to introduce this mutation into aviculture.

By the year 1954, 14 blue birds were known in captivity. Of these, four belonged to Dave West. With the death of the Duke of Bedford in the same year, his original pair of blue birds were sent to Keston Foreign farm where four more blues were raised from this pair.

A breeder from this farm named Edward Boosey also found a harlequin that was green and yellow. This bird had large yellow spots on the body and had tail feathers that were yellow in color along with flight feathers that were bright yellow. These birds did not become very popular in aviaries for a long time.

The first albino was raised in the year 1963 at Keston Foreign Bird Farm, but it did not survive for too long.

Even to this day, several cross breeds of Indian Ringnecks are being produced to create interesting color patterns. This is another contributing factor to the increasing popularity of the bird.

5. Distribution and habitat

The range covered by the Indian Ringneck natively is quite wide. They are found in a lot of tropical areas starting from the West of Africa, stretching all the way around India up to the southern foothills of the Himalayas. Their range of distribution includes Pakistan, Nepal, and Southern Vietnam. The Indian Ringneck, which is the most commonly seen sub species, is believed to have originated in the island of Sri Lanka at the Southern tip of the Indian subcontinent. They are the most commonly seen species in captivity.

In the native land of India and Sri Lanka, these birds are normally seen in wooded areas and in forests. This subspecies, however, is extremely adaptable and easily adjusted, even in areas that were inhabited by human beings primarily. This included urban areas, farms, agricultural areas and suburban areas. All these birds require to thrive is a food source and nesting sites.

Sadly, these birds were looked upon as pests in most of these areas because they targeted the agricultural areas for food, damaging most of the crop that was found there.

As we have seen, the Indian parakeet will inhabit any area where they can obtain ample food and safe nesting sites. This is true for just about any bird in the wild. In the case of Indian parakeets, the most preferred sites for nesting are cavities in trees. This is found in abundance in rural, suburban and urban areas across India and the native range of this bird.

As for food, they eat a variety of different types of seeds, flowers, grains, nuts, fruits and berries. This is one of the primary reasons why their populations are so abundant in the wild and in captivity. Their diet and roosting areas vary as per the region that they inhabit and the season. For instance, in Egypt, they will usually eat mulberry during the spring and dates when it is summer. They prefer to nest in palm trees and also eat from surrounding corn and sunflower fields.

In India, on the other hand, their primary source of food is cereal grain during the warmer months and pigeon peas when winter sets in. Indian Ringnecks are known to travel across several miles to find their food. They love to forage, which means they cause a lot of damage to farms and orchards, making them a pest in these regions.

Because of the ease with which they adapt, these birds have been introduced in different parts of the world. They are now seen in large populations in the USA, particularly in California, Florida and Hawaii. There are some established populations in Japan, Africa and the Middle East. The beauty of the Indian Ringneck is that although it is from a tropical range originally, the bird has also adapted to the cold conditions in Britain because of the easy availability of food in the countryside and the urban areas.

6. Feral populations of Ringnecks

A lot of Indian Ringneck parrots have been released across the globe, giving them a chance to thrive because of fewer predators and a wide range of food options available thanks to bird feeders as well as gardens in the suburbs. These birds get a lot of their preferred foods in these areas including fruits, berries, nuts, and seeds.

Because these birds were able to adapt to the cold conditions in the foothills of the Himalayas, it was quite obvious that they would also thrive well in the cold conditions in European countries.

Today, there are well-established feral populations in Japan, South Africa and several European cities. You will also find their stable populations in parts of the United States.

Besides this, there are a few small, but self-sustained populations in the parks of Ankara, Tripoli, Tunis and the northern parts of Tehran. You will also see them in Israel, UAE, Lebanon, Bahrain, Oman and

Qatar. The populations of these birds that are found in Australia are mostly made up of those that have escaped from captivity.

In European countries, the populations of these birds began to grow in the mid-20th century. They are mostly concentrated around London in the southwestern and western suburbs.

In London, these birds have regularly been spotted in Richmond Park, Crystal Palace Park, Battersea Park, Wimbledon Common, Hampstead Heath, Surrey, Greenwich Park and Berkshire. There is a large population of these birds that have come to be known as Kingston Parakeets in the southwest of London.

In the year 2000, the winter season brought in about 6000 birds around London in three different roosts. There are also a few flocks in Broadstairs, Margate, Kent and Ramsgate. In the North Eastern part of London, you will see these birds in Essex.

Besides this, you will see smaller feral populations that seem to establish themselves from time to time in areas like Greenbank Park, Studland, Dorset, Manchester, Kensington Garden and Sefton Park. Today, these birds outnumber the native birds in Britain and it has also been speculated that these birds can endanger the native species. Some efforts have been made to cull the populations of these birds. Recent reports, however, show that the urban populations of these birds have been on the rise steadily.

Indian Ringnecks have also been spotted in several areas in the Netherlands. Even in this part of the world, a large population of the birds resides in the urban areas including The Hague, Utrecht, Rotterdam and Amsterdam. As of 2010, the estimated population was about 10,000 birds, which is double the census that was taken just six years prior in 2004.

In Brussels, a population of these birds was released in the year 1974 by the owners of the Attraction Park at Atomium and Meli Zoo. They released the birds in order to make the city more colorful. Today, you will find an estimated 5000 pairs of these birds in Brussels alone.

These birds have also been spotted in Germany along all the urban areas such as Dusseldorf, Cologne, north Hamburg, Wiesbaden,

Heidelberg, Ludwigshafen, Bonn and along the Rhine. The populations add up to a few hundred in each of these areas.

In Europe, the other populations are concentrated around Paris and Rome and also in the Palatine Hill gardens, in trees around Janiculum and Trastevere, the Orto Botanico de Palermo, Villa Broghese, Lisbon, Barcelona and Genoa.

In these naturalized areas, one will mostly find hybrids that are intra-specific. This means that the hybrids are formed by breed two subspecies. There are also some inter-specific populations where these birds have bred with native species like the Alexandrine Parakeet.

While their feral populations are on the rise, it has been noted that the birds are diminishing in numbers in parts of South Asia where they actually originated. This is due to heavy pet trade. A lot of efforts have been made to restore the populations of these birds by setting them free from captivity. Still, the populations have significantly reduced, especially in India.

Feral populations of the Indian Ringnecks have been found in Japan. The Japanese began to own these birds as pets only around the 1960s. They were imported in large numbers for this reason. Some of these birds escaped, while others were released and their feral populations began to thrive round the 1980s in areas like Osaka, Tokyo, Niihata, Nagoya and Kyushu. Some of these groups did disappear over time, but a recent study revealed that there is a large population of Indian Ringnecks in the Tokyo Institute of Technology and also in China city and Maebashi.

In the areas that the birds have been introduced, they have affected wellness, economy and the natural biodiversity.

7. Personality

Indian Ringnecks have a reputation for being aggressive and nippy. They go through a phase that is called "bluffing" which we will discuss in the following chapters. This has caused several owners to believe that their pet is aggressive. However, for the most part, these birds are friendly and will make great pets.

They are very easy to tame provided that you are willing to give them the attention that they require. When the interaction with your parrot is restricted to feeding and cleaning time, they will quite naturally become detached and also unfriendly. With Indian Ringnecks, this switch in personality due to neglect happens quite rapidly.

It is a good idea to hand feed your bird from a young age to make them calmer around people. They will also be less nippy when they are accustomed to being handfed. You must also make it a point to interact with your bird for a few minutes everyday just to play a game or to simply pet your bird. Indian Ringnecks are not particularly great with cuddles. However, if you stroke the feathers in the direction of growth, they seem to enjoy it quite a bit.

The best thing about Indian Ringnecks is that these birds are extremely intelligent. They are able to learn new behavior from people just by observing. This is one of the main reasons why they are so great at mimicking human voices.

If you are willing to take the time to train your bird, you will see that they can learn to speak better than most other species of parrots. When they are about one year of age, Indian Ringnecks will begin to speak and pick up words. They are capable of learning as many as 250 words, which is the highest among parrots.

Their quality of speech, however, is not as clear as parrots that are larger. The ability to speak and the number of words that your bird learns depends upon the amount of time you are willing to spend with the bird. In fact, even though they will not cuddle, they will happily sit on your shoulder and arm all day. That is how much your Indian Ringneck loves to spend time with its owner.

These birds are extremely smart and need to be challenged mentally. In fact, they demand a good challenge, without which they even develop several behavioral issues. It is up to the owner to give them lots of complicated toys, teach them new tricks, play games with them and engage them in your own activities around your house.

The bond that your parrot will form with you is extremely strong. It has been observed that the bond formed by females is a lot stronger while the male seems to be a little more relaxed in his approach.

That said, these birds will also accept a flock quite willingly. So, even if you are the one that your bird is most strongly bonded with, it is recommended that other members of the family also interact with the bird, handle him regularly and also feed him. Indian Ringnecks, particularly the females, become very jealous when you show affection to other members of your family. To prevent this and any aggression towards that individual, having them interact with the bird is actually quite necessary.

During the phase of bluffing or in case of any form of bad behavior, ignoring the bird gives you the best results. They will display bad behavior as a means to seek your attention. Some amount of gentle dominance is good to make your relationship peaceful. You can also rely on positive reinforcement when the bird behaves in a manner that is acceptable to you.

These birds are very curious and will be up for just about any adventure. They will be demanding when it comes to attention. One more personality quirk with the bird is that they are very talkative. Sometimes, they will talk for hours on end. They can also be noisy in general, making whistling and screeching sounds from time to time.

If you are a first timer, you will need to learn as much about this parrot as you can before you decide to make the commitment. They are not ideal pets for children, as they are very sensitive by nature. Any sudden sounds or movements will spook them easily. They also tend to have night frights, which will make them thrash about in the cage when they are startled.

If you are ready to take on some challenges along with all the positives that come with owning an Indian Ringneck, you will be a great owner. It will certainly take up a good amount of your time, but given the companion you will find it will all be worth it!

8. Popular myths

You may hear several myths about the Indian Ringneck that will put you in two minds about bringing the bird home. In addition to that, it may also hamper your approach to care for your birds. Here are few popular myths that you need to know about:

They do not make good pets

This is a myth that is sometimes even propagated by breeders and experts. One of the reasons why this bird developed a bad reputation is because of a habit called bluffing. When you wean an Indian Ringneck, it is common for them to go through a phase that makes them excessively nippy.

This stage does not last too long. However, it can be very difficult for owners to put up with and often detours them. Think of this stage as dealing with a hormonal teenager who is extremely moody and mostly in a bad mood. This is a part of the bird's development and after it has passed, your bird will become tame and quite friendly. Make sure you do not let the bird test its limits too much with some dominance in this phase.

They like to be left alone for a long time

Being social is one of the most important traits of the Indian Ringneck. In the wild, a lot of their time is spent with their flock and with the mate that they choose for the breeding season. The mating behavior of this bird is responsible for this reputation. In the wild, the bird has been spotted alone at times. In addition to that, they are not monogamous like most parrots. This means that they will pick a different partner every breeding season.

However, these birds need your attention and fare very poorly when they are left alone. They also enjoy the company of other birds when they are introduced correctly to them.

Male Ringnecks learn to talk better than females

The gender of the bird does not determine how well they will learn to talk. Both the male and female birds will talk just as well as long as they are trained properly. Females also whistle quite well and learn to mimic different sounds when you spend time with them.

The possible cause for this rumor is the fact that male Ringnecks are usually preferred as pets. This is because the male is more colorful than the female, which makes the latter "less in demand". However, there is no difference in the talking abilities.

You have to remove hatchlings away from the mother before they can open their eyes to make them tame

This is a myth that you must never pay any heed to. The truth is that after they have hatched, Ringnecks are oblivious to the different aspects of their environment for almost 10 days. If you separate them early, the birds may end up alone sometimes. It is always better to hand raise birds in groups rather than alone.

In the wild, the mother bird actually comforts her baby and keeps the little one alone while the father is feeding him. If you keep a baby Ringneck alone, you will have to give it something to cuddle with. If not, the baby bird will continue to cry. For you to tame your bird, the only option is to make sure that he/she is socialized well and that he/she gets ample interaction with you.

Female Ringnecks are more aggressive than the male

This is another statement that has made female Ringnecks less popular. They are just as, if not more loyal than the male birds. They tend to form deep bonds with their owners. They also show you a lot of affection and will love to spend time with you.

With females, petting and cuddling is also a lot more acceptable than it is with the males. The only season when your female Ringneck will seem aloof is during the breeding season.

This is when their body has a rush of various hormones that makes them a little moody and also territorial. Make sure that you learn how to handle the bird during this time and also take the necessary precautions to avoid any accidents.

This behavior is common with any parrot, in fact. Whether it is an Amazon parrot or a Macaw, the female will become very territorial and moody during the breeding season. They will even target their mate during this season to get their way!

The color determines how good your pet will be

No one really knows how this myth came to be. One theory is that because males are more colorful and are assumed to be better behaved, people began to relate color to behavior. However, the color of the plumes or the gender of the bird does not determine how well your pet will interact with you. It all boils down to the efforts that you make to socialize your bird with more people and also how stimulated you keep your bird.

Now that you know everything that you need about the Indian Ringneck, the next step is to determine whether you can commit as much time as is needed to raise the birds correctly. If you think time is something you can spare, we will talk about the care that these birds need in the following chapters. That will help you be entirely sure about your possible pet bird.

Chapter 2: Buying a Ringneck and Being Prepared

When you decide to bring an Indian Ringneck into your home, the first thing that you need to check is whether it is legal to have a bird in your city or state. For instance, owning or breeding these birds in New Jersey is illegal and has been banned. This is because the birds have been considered an agricultural pest in several parts of the world.

The second thing that you need to check is whether you need a license to have a bird in your area. You can contact the wildlife authorities in your state to learn about the legal issues related to the Indian Ringneck. Once you have confirmed that it is legal to own the bird, the next step is to make sure that you find the right source to obtain a healthy pet for your home.

1. Choosing the right source

There are several options out there when it comes to bringing a Ringneck home. Because of their high demand as pets, there are several breeders and pet stores that will sell these birds. In this section, you will learn all about making sure that you are in the right hands when you choose the bird that will be your pet for several decades.

Pet Store vs. Breeders

For those who are looking for convenience, the pet store can seem like the perfect option when it comes to buying a bird. While that is certainly an option, you must make sure that the pet store endorses good care and ethical breeding of the birds. When you are looking for a parrot in a pet store, make sure that you look for the following:

- Clean cages.
- Well maintained birds.
- Hygienic bird rooms that are away from the other animals being sold.
- Clean food bowls and clean drinking water for the birds.
- Knowledgeable staff.
- Adequate quarantining of all birds.

It is true that breeders are hard to find because they usually live in areas that are on the outskirts or because they do not invest much in advertising. That said, there are several websites that will list reputable breeders in your vicinity. You can also look for recommendations from other parrot owners or from a veterinarian in your locality.

If you are choosing a breeder from the Internet, make sure that you visit their facility before you make any commitment. In any case, you must make sure you inspect the breeding conditions before you bring your bird home to avoid nasty surprises. There are a few advantages of seeking out an Indian Ringneck breeder:

- You will be able to actually see the conditions and the environment that the birds are raised in.

- You will be able to see the parents of the bird to rule out any chances of genetic issues.

- With most reputable breeders, you will be able to find a lot of information and support with respect to raising your birds.

It is always an advantage to buy your bird from a breeder because, unlike a pet store, the birds do not come in large lots from different facilities. When various birds from various locations are caged together, chances are that the risk of disease is very high. Breeders are also less expensive because they usually do not have to invest in large spaces, advertising and in hiring employees for their facility. This saving is passed on to those who buy from them.

Choosing a good breeder
When there is a demand for a certain breed of bird or animal, you will naturally see a rise in the number of people breeding them. While some of them are genuinely concerned about the welfare of their birds, there are others who are involved in it only for the commercial benefit. The latter may resort to unethical practices to increase the number of birds that are produced in each breeding season.

Today, with the Internet providing free advertising, there are several breeders listed when you look for one in your vicinity. You will probably find several websites that will show up with the name and location. It is best that you visit the aviary before you fall for cheap discounts or sales online.

Here are a few tips that will help you find a good breeder to buy your pet from:

- The breeder should have clean aviaries, which are not rusty and shabby.

- The food and water bowls should not have any bird feces in them.

- The birds must not have ruffled feathers or any deformities.

- Proper quarantining measures should be taken for any bird that is sick or suspected of carrying any illness.

- When you approach a bird, it should be curious. If it sticks to a corner on the floor of the cage, he/she is probably unwell.

- The breeder should be willing to answer all your queries with respect to the Indian Ringneck.

- A closed aviary system where birds from other flocks are restricted is a good option. The aviaries also insist that you wash your hands thoroughly or change your boots before you enter the premises where the birds are kept. This is the best option, as the risk of illness is very low.

You can look for recommendations from previous clients of the breeder if possible. A good breeder will also help you meet the birds that have been bought from him. If you want to look for as many options as possible, you can sign up for email lists and groups such as "abird4sale" which is quite popular in Canada with over 800 members. You can join these groups on popular online groups such as Yahoo. Through these groups, you can read testimonials, get newsletters and online magazines that will help you find the perfect breeder to source a healthy Indian Ringneck Parrot from.

What you must look for

There are a few things that are advantageous for bird owners to make sure that their birds are a perfect fit for their home. When you are buying a bird from a breeder or a pet store, here are a few things that you can look for:

Are the birds hand-raised?

Not too long ago, birds that were hand raised were not easy to find. You could probably find them with breeders, but not really in pet stores. Today, the picture is quite different, with hand-raised birds being the preferred choice. Even in pet stores, they are hand raised to make them tamer and more social when it comes to human beings.

Hand raised birds are those that have been removed when they are hatchlings and then raised by human beings. Some breeders and pet stores will co-parent with the parent birds, but the babies are not raised entirely by the parents.

This makes the bird people oriented. That way, you have a "pet" from the time the bird enters your home. The bird will probably even step up on your finger or arm without much hesitation. These birds are less likely to bite as well. They do not perceive you or your hand as a threat.

When you visit a breeder, make sure that you ask for birds that are hand tamed, unless you are willing to spend the time it requires to train the bird and make it tame. Breeders will not hand raise a bird most often because they do not have the time and the resources required. In most cases, these birds are shipped off to pet stores and are sold at much lower costs than one that is hand tamed.

You will pay a price for this with a bird that may not become as tame as you want it to be. It is possible to make them social, but it requires careful training and probably a few nips from time to time.

When you pick a bird that you want to take home, it is a good idea to insist that you handle it. Even with birds that have been hand raised, particularly with Indian Ringnecks that have a tendency to bluff, you will find them becoming nippy or skittish around people. This is a sign that the birds are not being hand tamed.

In most places, the bird will be handled only until the time he/she needs assistance to eat. Once the bird has been weaned, it will be left in the aviary with the other birds with very little human interaction. These birds are more oriented towards birds, in comparison to people. These birds will most often try to bite when you reach out for them.

Birds that have been weaned correctly and trained to be easy to handle will, no doubt, be more expensive. This is because of the effort involved in making them that way.

The younger you buy your bird, the better. That way, you will not only have a hand fed bird, but you can also make sure that he gets the attention that he needs after he has been weaned. Younger birds also adapt a lot faster than older ones. Please note: I shall now refer to the bird as 'he', although you may also own a female.

Should the bird be weaned?
Most avian experts and experienced pet owners will discourage you from buying a bird that has not been weaned. The period of weaning can be really stressful on the babies and if you try to move them in that time, it gets even worse.

Research with popular veterinary facilities reveal that birds that have been sold or moved just before they are weaned are at a higher risk of developing health issues. This risk is greater if you already have pet birds at home and you have to introduce the new one to them. This is because the immune system is compromised with stress. It is true that birds that have already been weaned and are capable of feeding on their own are stronger in terms of immunity.

If you are new to the world of parrots, hand feeding is not very easy. It is also risky. Even if you know of people who have been successful at doing so, it is best not to take a chance. It depends on the personality of the bird and each bird is different when it comes to hand feeding. Some are easier than others.

There is also room for a lot of error when you are new. For instance, the formula may be a little overheated. This can cause serious crop issues and irritation in the crop lining. As a result, the bird may develop many infections. This damage happens very fast between the time the baby has stopped eating and the food stops moving through the crop. You need some experience to recognize a possible problem.

If you have a breeder or a pet store trying really hard to sell you a baby bird that has not been weaned, they are possibly trying to save themselves the trouble. This is passed on to you, along with a high risk to the well being of the bird.

You will hear a lot of reasons, like the bonding between you and your bird will be better or that it will love you more. In the wild, birds do not form permanent bonds unless they reach adulthood and have reached the breeding age. In the case of the Indian Ringnecks, the fact that they are not monogamous also leaves you a lot of room to bond with your pet.

All you need to do is be willing to give the bird the time, train him, make sure that you feed him well and keep him healthy in order to form a strong bond. Ringneck parrots will form a strong bond with one owner in most cases but are a lot easier to adapt in comparison to any other parrot breed.

When you handle your potential pet bird, here are a few things you need to look for additionally:

Does the bird only show a strong bond for one person?
If the breeder is able to bond with the bird and no one else in the family is, for example his wife, then there are chances that the bird will show a dislike for women in general. This behavior can be altered, if you have the time for it. If not, you might want to look for a bird that is capable of bonding with others while maintaining one strong bond with one human. That is the safer option if you want to prevent accidents.

Is the bird prone to screaming or biting?
Very often, birds pick up bad behavior because people, unknowingly, reinforce them. For instance, giving the bird a treat to stop screaming or even giving him attention is a sign for the bird that this is acceptable to behave in that manner. While they pick these behavior patterns easily, it can be really hard to get rid of them.

You may notice that the bird is calm in the presence of new people but will soon show this behavior when he has adjusted to their presence. This is why it is best that you spend some time with your potential pet before buying one.

Remember, once you have brought the bird home, you need to own any behavior quirks. They are certainly changeable. With some birds it may take a few days while with others it can take several months or even years. If that is the type of commitment you are willing to make, then consider a pet parrot. This can hamper your relationship with the bird if you are not willing to work on it.

How old is the bird?
This is a really important question for you to ask. With store bought birds, you may not be able to know the exact age, but an approximation at the very least is necessary. With older birds, training them is definitely more challenging. With birds that are too young, you will have to make additional efforts to keep them healthy while the immune system builds to its full capacity. A young, weaned bird is best when you are not very experienced with parrots or if you do not have enough time.

How important is it for the bird to talk?
For some parrot owners, one that talks is a bonus, while for others, it is the sole reason for bringing a parrot home. The good news is that Indian Ringnecks are excellent talkers and will probably pick up on a few words without you trying too hard to teach them. However, if you want to make sure that your bird talks very well, then buying a bird that is younger is a good idea. If you find an older Ringneck who is still unable to mimic human speech (although it is quite unlikely), the probability of this bird learning is lower. That said, older birds do not rule out the ability to talk entirely. However, it will take more time and patience.

Signs of good health
With younger birds, the signs of diseases are very mild and almost absent. This makes it extremely hard to know if you are bringing home a healthy bird or not. In fact, Ringnecks hide illnesses very well even when they are older. If you are observant, you will be able to find a few warning signs that could imply that the bird is unwell or has some abnormalities. These signs include:

The condition of the feathers

If you are handed a small, fluffy baby bird, it does seem cute and you may even believe that it is how they are supposed to look. However, by the time a baby Ringneck has been weaned, he is practically the size of an adult. The bird is able to perch like an adult and also has fully developed feathers.

It is quite normal for a bird to have feathers that seem disheveled when they are younger, as baby birds tend to be hard on their plumes. However, the down feathers should not stick out in between the colored feathers and through them. This is a sign that the bird is plucking his feathers or that the parents are doing so.

Bad plumage is also a sign that the bird has been weaned too early or has some disease. There are several serious illnesses that will affect the feathers.

The activity level

If you notice that the bird is in a corner of the cage and continues to sleep even if you approach him, he is probably unwell. It is true that young birds sleep a lot more than adults. However, with anything that is interesting such as a new visitor, they will become alert. If you are unsure, visit the bird a couple of times more to see if the activity level improves.

Appearance of nostrils and eyes

In birds, infections ted to manifest in the form of an eye infection, a plugged nose, or blocked sinuses. If you notice that the eyes are cloudy or red or that the nostrils have some discharge, it is a definite sign of illness. If the infection is minor, it can be cured with simple medication. However, it is best that you wait for at least a week to check on the bird. You must ensure that this bird is quarantined even if he seems like he is in perfect health when you buy him.

The weight of the bird

The bird that you are planning to buy should neither be overweight, nor should it be undernourished. The keel bone, which is present near the belly just above the bird's legs, is a good indicator of the body condition of the bird.

In adult birds, the bone should be in line with the flesh and must not protrude. In the case of baby birds, it tends to protrude a little after they have been weaned because they are usually active and also because they may lose some weight after weaning. If you notice that the bone is jutting out by more than $1/8^{th}$ of an inch, the bird still needs to develop before you take him home. In the case of an adult bird, that is a sign that the bird is malnourished and that he may also have underlying health issues.

Even when you are certain that your bird is healthy, make sure that you get a health guarantee. You see, in birds, it is hard to tell if they are healthy or not immediately. Should you notice any issues after the purchase, a health guarantee will be useful.

Health guarantee

With a reputable breeder, a health guarantee is provided with every specimen that they sell. If the seller has a health guarantee, it is an indication of good breeding practice.

With birds, it is always reasonable to believe that the bird may not be in the best of health when you make a purchase. Should you have to return the bird, a health guarantee ensures that you get a full refund. It is best that you avoid breeders who do not provide a health guarantee.

Without a health guarantee, it is almost impossible for a buyer to prove that the breeder knew about the illness when he made a sale. With a written health guarantee, you can make up for this lack of legal protection on the part of the buyer.

A health guarantee works both ways. It protects a seller if the new owner is negligent, and it also helps the buyer in case the breeder did not disclose any disease that the bird could be carrying. There are a few conditions that every health guarantee contains:

- The health of your bird is guaranteed for a total of three days as long as the bird has been thoroughly examined by a certified Avian Vet. This is an expense that you need to take care of.

- Should the vet find any issues that make the health of the bird unsatisfactory, you need a written document that will state the issues.

- You must return the bird immediately for a full refund. The species and the band number of the bird must be mentioned in the document provided. The breeder will not reimburse the vet fees or any expense that you have to bear for transportation.

- In case the bird dies within 12 days of purchase, you need to make sure that a necropsy is conducted within 72 hours after the death of the bird. If you are not able to conduct the necropsy immediately, the body must be refrigerated until the tests are conducted.

- The reports of the necropsy should be sent to the veterinarian of the breeder and must include the species and the band number. If these reports prove beyond any doubt that the bird had any health issues that originated before the purchase, you will be able to get a full reimbursement or a replacement. Some breeders will also allow you a 6-month window, during which the death of the bird will ensure reimbursement, provided a proper necropsy is conducted.

- The breeder will not be held responsible for any expenses that you have to bear for these tests. You will also not hold the breeder liable if any bird from your existing flock develops any problem. It is mandatory to quarantine every new bird and if you do not do so, you cannot hold the breeder responsible.
- You must ensure that the bird has been quarantined adequately when you bring him home. He should be kept away from the other birds for at least 30 days before introducing him into the flock.

- If you already have other birds at home for a year or more, you will have to provide all the medical records of the bird and correct documentation for their health. It is possible that viruses that infect birds stay in a certain environment for many hours even after the bird has recovered fully.

- Negligence on the part of the owner does not make the breeder liable for any return or reimbursement. For instance, if you leave the bird in the car on a hot day or if you do not provide the bird with adequate food and care, you cannot hold the breeder responsible for any health issues or even death.

Of course, a health guarantee does not cover for any behavioral or psychological issues. It is your responsibility to make sure that you spend time with the bird to understand his behavior before you make the purchase.

Identifying the bird

With most breeders, a leg band is used to identify the bird that they are selling. These leg bands will help you get an accurate history of the bird that you are purchasing. Leg bands will also tell you how old the bird is.

It is a good idea to look for breeders who will provide leg bands, as you will get a lot of information about your bird.

There are usually two types of leg bands:

Open bands

These bands can also be used on adult birds, as they come with a clamp that closes them. There are two types of these bands. The first one is the European design, which is made of aluminum. It has a cross section that is rectangular and comes with a pin that holds it together.

The European band signifies that the bird was either bred in some European country or that it is meant for export. It can also mean that a bird that was caught in the wild was sent to Europe and then put up for export. With this band, the information that you get is limited, as you cannot figure out the age or the exact origin of the bird in question.

There is another type of band that comes with a cross section that is circular. These bands are mostly made of steel and are issued by the USDA for imported birds that are meant to be quarantined. They are also used by veterinarians to denote the gender of the bird after the sexing process.

With the quarantine bands you will see that there is a 3 number code that is preceded by a 3 letter code. The first letter denotes the state that the bird was imported into. These bands are usually applied when a large shipment of Indian Ringnecks is involved. These bands should fit every bird that has been sent in with the shipment. Therefore, they are made larger in size. In most cases, the bands many not be closed near the seam because they were too small to fit the birds legs.

Earlier, these import bands were removed by vets, as they could endanger the bird. The split end is easily caught in toys, cage bars or the rope and thread used in the cage. This makes the bird thrash around and even break his leg in the process. During that time, after the bird had been imported properly, there was no need to keep the band on.

Today, however, banding is mandatory to safely transport the birds across the borders of a state. Unless the safety of the bird is compromised, you cannot remove these bands.

When used for sexing, an open band is placed on the left leg in the case of females and on the right leg in the case of males. When these bands were used by vets, the number of letters were different, usually 2 or 4 to help one distinguish between the import band and the sexing bands.

Sexing bands will be closed properly at the split. Any band that does not close properly is probably not valid or authentic. Some breeders may just take the band off one bird's leg and put it on another to make you believe that surgical testing has been done.

Closed bands
These bands are also called breeder bands or seamless bands because they are used on captive bred birds. They are placed on the feet of baby birds. They are flat and come with a cross section that is rectangular.

For this band to fit properly, it needs to be used on baby birds before their eyes are open. That is when it will slide into place comfortably. On average. the bird will be between 10 and 14 days of age when this band is put on them, so they cannot be smuggled easily.

You have a number-letter code and also the year when it was applied and the country or the province that the birds were born in. There are different colors to signify the age of the bird with just one glance.

If a breeder is part of a club, the name of the club is engraved on it as well. Some clubs will use a logo or symbol. You can trace these bands back by contacting any local breeder.

If the band is sourced from a particular company, it is harder to trace but it can be personalized as the breeder wants.

There are very rare instances of closed bands that are not authentic. You will sometimes find that the band is so large that you can just squeeze it right off the foot of the adult bird. The codes are also suspicious with just some number and no other information. These breeders do not want their aviary to be identified. The reasons for this are quite obvious.

Of course, there are several cases when the birds are bred perfectly but are not banded. This is when the breeder is simply unaware of the advantage of banding. The breeder is probably a newcomer who has been unable to source the bands. They may have also missed the right age to band the babies, after which the foot is just too large.

Some breeders just do not believe in banding, as they consider it harmful to the bird. However, no instance of injury has ever been reported due to a breeder band. If possible, get a baby who has a band on his leg. In case he is not banded, you can ask the breeder why that happened and can also ask to meet the clutch from which the bird has been picked. If all the birds are healthy, then your bird is also in good condition.

One bird or a pair?
This is a common question with first time parrot owners. The truth about parrots is that they do not need a cage mate if they are able to form a good bond with their owner. In fact, with Ringnecks this is even more applicable. These birds do not need the company of another bird of the opposite gender.

That said, if you do decide to buy a pair of parrots, make sure that they are of the opposite genders. Two males or two females in one cage can get very territorial. Even with a pair of the opposite gender, keep an eye on the birds to make sure that they are compatible. Birds that have been raised together are the safest bet. It is also possible for the female to become territorial and aggressive when she is hormonal.

A pair of birds is ideal if you do not have enough time for your birds, as they will keep each other company. In that case, it is possible that your pets will not be as strongly bonded to you as they are to each other.

If you decide to buy just one parrot, you need to make sure that he is mentally stimulated and has enough interaction with you on a daily basis. That will help the bird stay healthy and happy even without a cage mate. Make sure he has lots of toys such as puzzles and chewable toys for the best results.

Adoption
There are several rescue shelters that are working consistently to make sure that parrots that have been rescued or surrendered are able to find forever homes. They give you the option of fostering or adopting these birds.

With most of these organizations, a complete assessment of the family who will be taking the bird is mandatory to ensure that they are compatible. You will also be able to attend several in-house training programs that will educate you about providing proper care for the bird you bring home.

With parrots, their long life can be a bane. Some owners are unable to sustain the care that they provide or may just run out of patience with an adolescent Ringneck that is a little difficult to handle.

There are other birds that have been abandoned by breeders because they were unable to keep up with the demands of a stringent breeding program. Either way, a parrot does tend to become very lonely and can even develop mild to serious behavioral issues when they are abandoned. This is why it is very important to educate yourself about the bird before you decide to take one home, especially from a shelter.

Traits of a good shelter
Since the birds at shelters are already under a lot of stress, they need very good care. Without that, there are chances that the bird's condition will deteriorate with time. He may also contract several

infections, as his immunity is compromised. With a good shelter, you will get all the support that you need in order to raise your rescued bird correctly.

You can look for local shelters online. Chances are that you will find many of them in your vicinity. Here are some guidelines to help you choose a good shelter to adopt a parrot from:

- Every bird that is entered in this program should be checked thoroughly by an avian vet.

- Following that, the bird should be quarantined for at least 30 days off site. This means that the bird should be kept far away from the birds at the shelter.

- Once the bird has been removed from quarantining, it must be allowed to socialize with the volunteers and also with people who are looking to adopt.

- Facilities that provide a trainer are ideal, as they can help the bird work through various issues that are faced by the bird due to the transition and also abandonment.
- The facility should allow you to spend as much time as you need with the bird that you want to take home.

- If you are new to the world of parrots, the shelter should be willing to provide you with as much information as you need. In fact, with many facilities, there are regular classes that you are encouraged to attend before you choose to adopt an Indian Ringneck.

The process of adoption
Each shelter will have its own unique set of rules for everyone who wants to adopt a bird from them. However, there are some general rules that apply to almost every facility that you choose to adopt a bird from:

- You will have to fill in an application form with all your personal details.

35

- Some facilities will require you to attend a minimum number of classes before you can become eligible for adoption. If the history of the bird demands more attention, you may be asked to take additional classes.

- You must spend some time bonding with the bird that you choose. In some facilities, a minimum of three visits is mandatory. You will not be allowed to handle the bird unless you have finished at least one class. You can only handle the bird when staff members are present. Therefore, it is best that you make an appointment before you visit your bird.

- A complete physical exam of the other birds in your home might be necessary. This must be done by a certified avian vet. The goal of these examinations is to rule out psittacosis before taking the new bird home.

- A home visit is a must with every facility. They will also need the cage to be approved. So, you will have to invest in the cage before the bird comes home. In some facilities, there is a restriction on how far the potential adopters can reside from the shelter.

- You will have to pay an adoption fee that ranges from $30-$100 or £15-£50 based on the medical attention or other care that the bird required while at the facility.

Only when you have completed all these procedures will you be allowed to take the bird home. Even then, there are some conditions that you need to guarantee to be eligible for adoption:

- You will not use the bird for any breeding purposes.

- The bird should never be taken out of the house without a cage or a harness at least.

- The bird should be kept in an environment that is 100% smoke free.

- The bird should be examined annually to be a vet approved by the facility.

- The bird should be given a balanced diet that includes all the foods that are part of the natural diet of the Indian Ringneck.

- You must allow follow up visits by the authorities at the facility.

- In case you are unable to keep the bird for any reason, it will be surrendered to the facility that you adopted it from.

These rescue shelters put in a lot of work with each bird that is rescued. That is why they are extra cautious about whom the birds are given to. Some of them will not let you have a bird if there are aggressive pets at home or even if there is a child at home who are is very young.

You also have a limitation on how many parrots you can adopt each year. Even after all the work, they have the right to decline the application. If they do so, you can try again and make sure you fit into their criteria of a good adopter.

2. Housing the Indian Ringneck

If you are adopting the bird, you need to make sure that you have the housing ready. In any case, if the housing enclosure is in place, you will find it much easier to help your bird make the transition.

There are a few requirements that you need to fulfill to make sure that the cage is safe and appropriate for your bird. After all, the bird will be spending a lot of time in the cage and it should be a space that is a positive environment for the bird.

Choosing the right cage

With Indian Ringnecks, it is essential to remember that these birds are extremely active. This means that they need a lot of room to move around and play. You must also choose a cage that is convenient to clean and also easily dismantled to make sure that you can keep it hygienic and well maintained. The cage should be large enough to house the bird along with accessories like toys and perches.

The rule of thumb when it comes to choosing a cage for an Indian Ringneck is that you need to get the largest one that you can afford. Most often people forget to consider the tail when measuring the size of the bird's cage. You need to make sure that the tail does not stick out once the bird has been placed in it. If your Ringneck is able to do the following, then the cage is large enough:

- He is able to flap his wings.

- He is able to spread his wings in all directions without them touching the cage bars.

- He can easily hop from one perch to the other and even play with his toys without the tail or feathers getting stuck in between the bars.

- He is able to turn around easily.

The shape of the cage is very important. Round cages do look very fancy but they are extremely impractical. Since the cage tends to wrap around the bird's body when he moves around, it can cause damage to the feathers. The bars come in the way of the bird when he fans his tail or flaps his wings, making it hard for him to stay balanced.

With round cages, you also do not have enough room for the toys and the perches. Even if you buy one that is large enough for two perches, chances are that the one on the bottom gets a lot of bird feces on it. The perches also may cross over making it difficult for the bird to enjoy either one.

Because a round cage does not have corners, stretching the wings and climbing will become hard. In addition to that, round cages do not come with any grill on the bottom to keep the poop out of the bird's way. Even when the bird is out of the cage, he will have no place to sit because the top is slippery and solid. This leads to a dark and dingy environment within the cage as well.

It is also difficult to put any substrate in a rounded cage because of the round bottom. No substrate will fit perfectly or line the bottom well.

In the case of a rectangular or square cage, the width and depth is greater than the height. Since the height of the cage does not interfere with how much space the bird gets in the cage, it is the better bet. There are a few benefits of tall cages, which include more room for perches, hanging toys and also more space for the bird to climb.

The spacing and the thickness of the bar is another aspect that you want to consider. It should be narrow enough to prevent the head from getting caught, as that leads to feather damage and serious injuries. The spacing should be just enough for the feathers to get through easily in case they accidentally get out. That way the bird can pull them back in without getting hurt. In the case of the Indian Ringneck, a cage with bars spaced at $3/4^{th}$ of an inch is ideal.

The cage should have a door that will allow you to get your hand in comfortably. This makes it easy for you to handle the bird. It will reduce any stress to the bird in case he needs to be retrieved. Ideally, a cage with three doors works well with Indian Ringnecks. That will give you two doors to get the food and water bowls in and out. The third door will serve as the one that the bird will use when he wants to get in or get out.

Make sure that the doors have a good clip so that the bird is secure. These clips will not move even slightly after they have been locked, preventing any escapes.

The cage will require a tray on the bottom. This will collect any wasted food or seed husks. Remember that the tray will get dirty very easily and that you must clean it at regular intervals. Avoid any cage bottom that will require wood shavings or cob bedding. This can become a harboring area for several microbes if not maintained well.

There must be a grill above the cage to make sure that the waste that is collected in it, be it food or bird droppings, does not come in contact with the bird.

Make sure that you consider the material that the cage is made of. It should have a seal of non-toxic paint. If this is not available, the cage can become rusted in no time, leading to illnesses related to metal poisoning.

Brass cages should be avoided as they contain zinc, which is highly toxic to birds. The ideal options would be cages that are made from stainless steel or ones that are powder coated. These cages also last for a longer time.

Make sure that you invest in the cage wisely. While used cages may be cheaper, they may have issues like rust that can be harmful. This is a one-time investment that will go a long way in ensuring that your bird is secure and free from health issues.

Placing the cage correctly

Once you have chosen the perfect cage for your Indian Ringneck, make sure that you place it correctly in order to avoid any stress to the bird. There are a few guidelines that will help you make sure that the placement of the cage is perfect for your beloved Indian Ringneck.

Place the cage against a wall

It is natural to assume that a cage that is placed near a window or in the middle of the room will give the bird a lot of things to look at. However, with too many visual cues, the bird may actually feel threatened and stressed.

In the wild, Indian Ringnecks will choose areas that are shielded such as tree cavities to make sure that their young are safe. The cage should resemble this natural habitat in order to keep the bird as comfortable as possible.

If your bird happens to look at something stressful such as a hungry cat when he is looking out the window, he will be startled quite easily. The bird will not be able to conceal the distress, especially when he is sexually mature and aware of his position as a prey animal.

You can make sure that your bird does not feel threatened constantly by finding an area in your home where the cage can be placed against the wall. With this cover on one side, the bird will get an immense sense of security.

For the bird to have enough sunlight and also a view of the world outside, you can place the cage in a manner that a window is partially visible.

Choose areas where temperatures fluctuate less
A cage that is placed against a window is also recommended because temperatures can fluctuate in these areas. If there is a draft, winters can get too cold for the bird. If the cage is placed near direct sunlight, it can get pretty warm. This may lead to overheating in your bird.

Of course, the temperature inside your home is bound to vary all day long. Sadly, Indian Ringnecks do not have many options to adjust to this. So, choosing a location where the temperature is somewhat constant can be very beneficial to your bird.

This means that your birdcage should not be placed near an air-conditioning vent or a heating vent. Areas such as the kitchen where temperature will fluctuate quite drastically should not be chosen to keep the cage. This can have very unhealthy consequences for your beloved bird.

Keep the cage at chest level
The height at which the cage is placed will also play a very important role with respect to your bird's behavior. Ringnecks should not be kept in cages that are placed on the ground. In their natural habitat, a Ringneck Parrot prefers to fly or climb. When they are placed too close to the ground, it is natural for them to feel threatened.

Make sure that the cage is not placed at a height where the bird is below your eye level. This will put you in the position of a predator every time you interact with your bird. Quite naturally, the bird will feel extremely anxious and stressed all the time.

At the same time, keeping your bird above the eye level will give him a false sense of superiority. Since Ringnecks are known to be territorial and dominant, this can have adverse effects on the way the bird responds to you. This can lead to several behavioral issues with your bird, such as nipping and aggression.

Keeping the cage at chest level is the best option. This makes the personal interaction with your bird more relaxed and easy. The bird will also not feel insecure or threatened. With this type of placement, the chances of behavioral issues are also greatly reduced.

The cage should not be close to health hazards
Every home is unique but what is common is that all homes have some hazards that can have negative impacts on the bird's health. Rooms like the kitchen and bathroom tend to have several chemicals, hot surfaces and also objects with sharp edges. In these rooms, temperature and humidity can also change constantly.

Make sure that the area that your birdcage is placed in is free from air fresheners and cleaning solutions. These items contain several chemicals that can be toxic to birds.

You must also never place a bird in a room where the chances of the windows and doors being open are high.

Final cage placement checklist
To sum it all up, here is a complete checklist to make sure that the cage is properly placed.

Never:

- Place the cage right in front of a window.

- Keep the bird in a room that has drastic temperature and humidity fluctuations.

- Place the cage near A/C or heating vents.

- Place the cage such that it is too close to the ground or above eye level.

- Place the cage in a room that may have potential hazards that can compromise the well-being of the bird.
-

Always:

- Place the cage with a wall on one side to make your bird feel secure.

- Place the cage in a room that you use often to allow more interactions with your bird.

- Choose an area that will allow your bird to socialize with other birds in your home or even pets.

- Place the cage at chest or eye level.

- Keep an eye on any possible signs of stress that can be related to the placement of the cage.

In order to adjust to a new environment, your parrot will need to establish himself. That is why choosing the perfect location is ideal to avoid changing it too many times. This can make your bird stressed and disoriented. That is why bird enthusiasts lay so much emphasis on the correct placement of the birdcage.

Toys and accessories for the cage
Accessories and toys are not optional when it comes to Indian Ringnecks. These are extremely necessary to keep the bird mentally stimulated and to convert the environment within the cage into an engaging one. There are three accessories that are essential inside the cage:

- **Food and water bowls:** The most important criteria with the food and water bowls is that they must be easy to clean. That way, you can make sure that there is no contamination that can lead to serious health issues in the bird.

  You can have two stainless steel bowls with one serving as the water bowl and the other as the food bowl. Some pet stores will recommend a water bottle for your birdcage. This is a good idea if the bird is unwell and has any illness that is related to water contamination. Second, if you find bird droppings in the water bowl regularly, you may want to switch to a bottle.

Make sure that the bowls are deep enough for the bird to pick the food up comfortably. The water bowl should not be large enough for the bird to bathe in it. If you see that your bird has the urge to bathe in the water bowl, you can keep a spare one. The bird will then dedicate one water bowl to drink from and the other one to bathe in on his own.

Some cages come with a holder or a clip that will keep the food and water bowls in place. This is a feature that you must look for in the cage to make sure that you do not have a mess in the cage that you will have to clean up often.

- **Perches:** Perches act as the resting area for your bird. Climbing the perch and even standing on it can be a great form of exercise for your bird.

If you have enough room, it is a good idea to have multiple perches that are sized differently. If they are all the same in terms of diameter, your bird will soon be bored out of his mind.

There are different types of perches that you can choose from. They are:

- Natural perches: Natural perches that have been cleaned and sanitized properly are possibly the best option. You can use eucalyptus branches, for example. Before you place a natural perch in the bird's cage, make sure that it is washed thoroughly enough to remove any pathogens and pesticides. You must also do a good amount of research on the type of tree branch that you are choosing to ensure that it is not poisonous for the bird. Some trees like pine, cherry and oak should be avoided. The advantage with natural perches is that they will help the bird develop stronger leg muscles and feet.

- Rope perches: These perches are extremely flexible and are a lot of fun for the bird. Since the perch is bendable, you can even shape it differently each time to make it fun for the bird. The advantage of the soft surface of the rope perch is that it does not irritate the feet of the bird. They provide a different texture and also a different thickness among the perches that you are using. You need to make sure that the rope perches are made of cotton or sisal threads that have been twisted tightly in place. Any fray thread can lead to snagging of the bird's feet.

- Plastic perches: These are possibly the most economic option when it comes to perches. They are sturdy and give the bird a good place to roost and land. The advantages with plastic perches is that they are very easy to clean and durable. But, you need to make sure that the surface is not too smooth. That makes it hard for the bird to get a firm grip on the perch. The biggest drawback with this type of perch is that plastic can be extremely harmful if the bird ingests it. So you need to make sure that there aren't any small parts that are easy to swallow.
- Dowel perches: Normally, the dowel perch will come with the cage of the bird. It usually contains a wooden base that supports the perch. This makes sure that birds of any size can find perfect grip and support on this type of perch. The material is very easy to clean. It is also a comfortable shape for your Indian Ringneck. If the cage comes with a dowel perch, you will have to get another type of perch to make sure that there is some variety of shape and surface for more mental stimulation for your bird.

- Cement perches: These are hard surfaces and are very commonly seen. The advantage with this type of perch is that the nails of your bird will remain trimmed. That way, you do not have to go through the ordeal of trimming the nails of your pet bird. You must, however, make sure that the bird has a softer alternative within the cage if you are using a cement perch. If the bird uses a surface this hard for long hours, the feet will not only hurt, but the bird will also feel extremely uncomfortable.

You can try different perches for your bird and see what suits him the best. When you decide upon the type of perch that you want, there are a few things to keep in mind when hanging it in the cage:

- The perch should always be near the food and water bowls. Ideally, you should place it in front of the bowls so that they are easy to reach. However, the perch should never be directly above them to prevent any droppings in the food and water.

- The perch should be installed in such a way that the tail of bird does not touch the walls of the cage or the floor.

- The cable or wire that you use to hang the perch should not intertwine and should not have any frays. This can cause injuries to the bird.

- There must be multiple perches at different levels but not so many that the bird is unable to fly inside the cage.

- The perch must be scrubbed regularly to prevent any dried feces or dirt.

The perch is more than just a resting area for the bird. It is the place where the bird will sharpen his beak, remove pieces of food that are stuck in the beak and is also the ideal place for the birds to socialize if you have a flock. Therefore, make sure that you invest in a good perch that is comfortable and durable. It will keep your bird fit and mentally stimulated as well.

- **Toys:** A good amount of toys in the cage will make sure that your bird does not get bored. Without stimulation, you will have a bird that may develop health and behavioral issues. When you are not around, the bird is on his own. This is when he will need to entertain himself and toys are essential for that. There are a few things to consider when choosing toys for your bird:

- First, the toys must have different textures. This helps to stimulate the feet and the mouth of the bird.

- Second, they should be extremely colorful. Indian Ringnecks can see a much wider spectrum of colors.

- Third, they must have different sizes to keep the bird mentally stimulated.

- Fourth, toys with different tastes will also fulfill the urge of the bird to chew and will stimulate the palate.

- Lastly, the toys must offer some challenge to the bird. This includes ladders and puzzles. Any toy that involves problem solving can be very interesting to your bird.

There are different types of toys that you can choose from. There are four main categories that they are divided into. Make sure you have at least one from each category. The types of toys available are:

- Chewable toys: When you put these toys into the cage, expect the bird to chew it all up immediately and shred it into pieces. With these toys, the birds feel a sense of accomplishment. It is almost the same feeling that you get when you have done the impossible at work!

  The parrot sees the shreds of the toy as the fruit of his labor. Of course, this activity is a lot of fun. It also keeps the bird's beak in great shape. You can find chewable toys that are made of different material such as leather, hardwood, soft wood, paper and also soft plastic.

- Foraging toys: These toys are the latest addition among parrot toys. They are extremely fun and will bring back the foraging instinct of the bird. When you hide treats in these toys, the bird will begin to look for it immediately. This is a challenging toy that makes the bird apply his mind well.

  Most foraging toys are made from material that cannot be easily destroyed. These toys have the potential to become you bird's favorite in no time. Then there are other foraging toys that are meant for the bird to rip and tear. With foraging toys that are indestructible, boredom will set in once the bird figures out how the toy works.

There are alternatives like wrapping the treats in recyclable paper or newspaper and letting your bird shred it into pieces to find the treat.

- Long lasting toys: Toys that are long lasting or advertised as "last forever" can be a great addition to the bird's collection of toys. These toys are durable and will usually come in the form of puzzles that your bird will love. While these are ideal for larger birds, you can also get ones that are size appropriate for your Indian Ringneck. These toys are made from PVC or acrylic material. The birds will love the components that are included in these toys and will benefit from twisting and turning it around.

- Physical stimulation toys: One of the best examples of this type of toy is a swing. The bird will have to use his muscles to climb up on the swing and then balance himself on it. When the bird learns how to use the swing, you will actually see him move back and forth to create movement on the swing.

With toys like swings, the muscle coordination improves. It also makes it possible to prevent conditions like muscle atrophy. With some of these toys, you will also have chewable toys that hang down, giving your bird the best of both worlds.

It is a good idea to introduce the toys one after the other and then rotate them every week. That way, the bird will have something new to look forward to each time and will not be bored easily.

If you notice that the bird is scared of a toy or is easily spooked by new colorful toys, it will help to keep the toy outside the cage for a few days before putting it in. That way, your bird will have a chance to get used to the toy first.

Avoid any toy that is painted or contains chemical dyes. Dyed leather, especially, can contain several toxins. There should not be any small parts that can be swallowed by the bird. Scatter the toys around and never place them one on top of the other. That will help you keep them cleaner for longer.

The toys that you choose should be appropriate for the size of your Ringneck. Something too small can be swallowed and something too big will not let the bird have a good time. While it is a good idea to get your bird as many toys as you can, make sure that the cage is not stuffed with toys, making it inconvenient for the bird to move around.

Any toy that is broken or damaged should be replaced immediately to prevent injuries.

Maintaining the cage
After your bird has been introduced to his new housing area, you need to make sure that you keep it in top condition to prevent harboring sites for pathogens. A good and clean cage is also essential for the mental well being of your bird. Ringnecks hate to live in dingy and dirty cages and will develop several health issues.

On a daily basis, you will have to clean out the food and water bowls. The substrate should also be changed every day to prevent any damp areas within the cage.

Every fortnight, it is recommended that you take all the toys and perches out of the cage and give them a thorough wash. Washing them with baking soda solution or diluted vinegar can help disinfect them and really clean them out. That said, a toy must immediately be washed if you notice bird poop or any debris on it. Dry them out in the sun completely. Sunlight also acts as a mild disinfectant. Of course, you do not want damp toys to attract fungal and bacterial growth.

Washing the cage thoroughly is a good idea once a month or more depending upon how messy your bird is. The bottom line is that dried food and feces should never be found stuck on the floor or the bars of the cage. Even if you are unable to thoroughly wash the cage, make sure that you wipe down areas that have any food or feces deposits.

Before you wash the cage, place your bird in a different carrier. Then, you can rinse out all the toys, perches and cage accessories and let them dry.

Then, rinse the cage with plain water. You can use a mild soap if needed. Make sure that you wash it out completely to prevent any residual soap in the cage.

You can also spray the cage with baking soda solution and scrub out any dirt or debris. Once you have all the dirt out of the way, rinse the cage thoroughly and allow it to dry in the sun. Make sure that you check the floor, the bars and the roof of the cage before you put your bird back in. They must all be clean and free from any protrusions or sharp edges.

Then, you can place the toys and accessories back in the cage and put your bird back in his fresh as new home!

3. Parrot proofing your home

Your home should be a safe environment for your bird. That can be achieved when your home is parrot proofed to prevent any chances of injury or accidents in your home. Here are some useful tips to parrot proof your home:

- Make sure that the cage is not placed on a hard surface. Should your bird have a fall, he can sustain serious injuries.

- The windows should be marked or should have a safe object hanging in front of it. That way, you will not have any instance of the bird flying into the windows and hurting himself.

- Electrical wires should be enclosed completely. There should not be any loose wires near the cage, especially on the floor. If someone accidentally trips on it and tips the cage over, it can be bad news for your bird.

- All the toilet lids and any water container in your home should be covered. There have been several reports of Ringneck parrots and other species of parrots drowning accidentally.

- The parrot cage should be away from the kitchen. There are fumes, especially those released by Teflon pans, which can be toxic for your bird. Prolonged exposure to these fumes can cause serious health issues.

- It is best to have a kitchen with a door that can be closed every time the parrot is out of the cage. Hot stove tops and utensils are the number one cause of injuries in birds.

- Do not have doors that can close automatically. There are chances that your bird will get caught in between when the door is shutting.
- Table fans should be kept out of the bird's way. Make sure that all fans, table or ceiling, are off when your bird is let out of the cage.

- Always check doors and windows when you leave your home. You do not want your bird to get away if you leave the house with one of them open.

- Make sure you check if a certain plant is toxic to your bird or not when you place it near the cage of the bird.

- The cage doors should have a secure lock. A simple latch does not hold a Ringneck back, as they will soon figure out how to let themselves out. Do not forget that you are dealing with a very intelligent bird.

The safer the environment, the less stressed your bird will be. You will also not have to worry about untoward incidents that will leave your bird with serious injuries. Even after all the precautions have been taken, make sure that you never leave the bird out of his cage without proper supervision.

4. Considerations before you bring home a Ringneck

After you have made all the preparations, make sure you ask yourself a final set of questions to be completely sure that you are ready for a parrot. If you think that a parrot is not as big a responsibility as a dog or a cat, then you need to reconsider your decision of being a parrot parent. Make sure you think about the following:

Do you have enough time for the bird?

A lot of people look for a bird that does not need too much attention or one that is "low maintenance". If you are one of them, you must reconsider having any parrot. They need a lot of quality time and it is better if each member in your family can spend some time with them. Only if you are willing to make that commitment should you get an Indian Ringneck.

Are you prepared for the expenses?

The bird itself can cost you anything between $150- $800 or £70-500 depending upon whether you choose to adopt the bird or buy a certain hybrid. Then you have to invest in a cage that can cost between $100- $500 or £60- £200. Including other expenses such as the food, bedding, veterinary visits, toys and other supplies, you will need to shell out close to $500-600 or £200-300 per annum. Of course, this does not include any medical emergency that can just shake the whole budget up. Only when you know that you have the funds for regular and emergency expenses should you own a parrot.

Did you know that a parrot can be very messy?

From regurgitating stick food, coating the beak with smashed food and shaking it all around the cage or just leaving feather dander everywhere, parrots can make quite a mess. Of course, you cannot rule out the fact that they poop around the clock. Sometimes, even after the bird has been potty trained, there are chances that he will poop on your favorite clothes or on expensive upholstery. If you are very meticulous about your housekeeping, be prepared for a big mess when you bring the parrot home. If you do not want a mess, you should not have a parrot.

Is the parrot meant to be a gift?

When the holiday season arrives, we all get a little carried away and try to spoil our loved ones with anything that they want. But, if you are giving away a parrot as a gift, think twice. Is the other person ready for the responsibility? Are you sure that the parrot fits into their schedule? Do they have the financial resources to care for the bird? If you are not sure, then do not gift an Indian Ringneck.

Even if you think that the person is going to be able to do all of the above, make sure that you also arrange for behavioral, nutritional and environmental counseling with a vet or with rescue facilities that have them. If your loved one is reluctant to attend these, then you have a reason to take the parrot back and make sure it gets a good home.

Are you considering a pet for your child?
A Ringneck is not a good pet for a child. Normally, pet shops and breeders do not sell a bird to a child because of several unpleasant experiences. The fact is that even if your child is generally very responsible and is actually saving up to buy a parrot, the bird may not be a safe bet for the child. They are easily startled and can nip in defense. As we saw before, an Indian Ringneck in the bluffing stage can be a threat to the child's safety.

In addition to that, there is also a chance that the child may lose interest eventually. This will put all the responsibility on you. If you are unable to fulfill that, you will have a neglected bird or even worse, a bird that will eventually be abandoned.

Is the parrot meant to be a companion to another bird?
Sometimes, when we are unable to give our pets as much time as they need, the guilt makes us believe that they need a friend of their own kind. If that is the purpose of bringing a Ringneck parrot home, then it is useful to know that no matter how many birds you have, they will all need time and attention from you.

Are you ready to make different kinds of foods for your parrot?
Just a bowl of birdseed in the corner of the cage is not good enough. It will lead to a lot of health and behavioral issues. When you bring a Ringneck home, you also take on the responsibility of chopping vegetables and fruits, making sprouts and making special pellet mixes that are nutritious for your bird. Unless you have the time for this, you should not bring a parrot home.

Do you know that a Ringneck lives long?
In captivity, Indian Ringnecks live for at least 30 years on average. Some live as long as 50 years. This means that there is a chance that the generation after you will also have to take care of the parrot depending on how old you are when you buy a parrot. In addition to

53

that, do you think that you can plan that far ahead? What if your job gets more demanding or you have to move? What about when you have a newborn in the house? Will you be able to manage your parrot through all these life changes?

Each year several parrots are abandoned because their owners did not expect so much work. They deserve to be in a home where you not only prepare to bring the bird home but also prepare for the future and ensure that the bird gets a good life.

Chapter 3: Welcome Birdie

Your home is a brand new environment for the bird. It will take some time for you to help him get adjusted to this new environment.

1. Helping the bird adjust

Transitioning from his old home to the new one is stressful for the bird. The more you try to coddle the bird, the harder it is. The trick is to ease him in and let him learn about everything around him and get familiar with them on his own. Ringnecks are extremely observant and will learn a lot on their own.

The ride home

This is certainly the most stressful part. A vehicle such as a car is probably something that the bird has never experienced before. So, it is up to you to make it as comfortable as possible.

First, get a secure carrier that is large enough for the bird to spread his wings comfortably. Lining the cage with ample substrate will help keep the cage dry even if the bird does have any accidents during the drive home.

Make sure that you do not interact with the bird. Just place the carrier in a secure position. Make sure that it is free from any cold drafts during the drive. The temperature in the car should be maintained at room temperature.

Do not talk to your bird. It is also recommended that you do not turn any music on. If you have other passengers in your car, keep your interactions limited with them as well. Let him rest. Keep an eye on the bird. If it is a long drive, make sure you stop every 20 minutes or so to give the bird some water. Stopping the car will give the bird some time to relax. A moving carrier is definitely very stressful for the bird. A blanket on one side of the carrier will give your bird a resting spot and a place to hide if he feels scared.

If you see that the bird is huddled up in a corner, it is possible that he is afraid. Do not try to reach for him or comfort him. Vomiting can be avoided by feeding the bird about an hour before you depart. It is good to offer treats but not in large quantities.

Once the bird is home, if he still seems to run for cover or if he remains in the corner on the floor, consult your vet. In any case, a thorough check up by a vet is recommended after the bird is brought home.

First day at home

Place the carrier with the door facing the door of the permanent housing area. Sometimes the bird will hop right in when you open the door. If he takes time, let him get into the new cage at his own pace. If he seems restless, using a treat to lure him into the permanent cage is advisable.

Once the bird is in the new cage, close the door securely and let the bird be. On the first day, it is mandatory for you to keep your distance from the bird. Limit your interactions to feeding and changing the substrate for a few days.

Make sure you do not invite people over to see your new bird just yet. New faces can be stressful for the bird. Talking to the bird is to be avoided, as new voices are also too much for the bird on the first day.

There will be no loud music or television at a high volume on your bird's first day at home. Let the bird observe you and your whole family from the cage. You can go about your daily routine as is. The more he observes, the calmer he will get.

As the days pass

You can slowly begin to interact with your bird as he seems more comfortable in his new home. Start by just placing your hand on the walls of the cage and let him breathe in your scent.

A soft hello and goodbye is good enough for the first few days. Even if the bird is hand tamed, you must not try to reach out for him for at least a week or so. This time period varies from one bird to the other.

Watch the body language of the bird. If his posture is erect and laid back, he is possibly adjusted to the new home. When you place your hand on the cage, the bird must comfortably approach it. That means that he is learning to trust you. If he moves away or seems unsure, do not force him by calling or talking to him. He will eventually loosen up.

Never tower over the cage. Make sure that the bird is always at your eye level when he is new to your home. When you are at a higher level, he will perceive you as a threat. That will make the process of building trust a lot harder.

The ease with which a bird gets accustomed to a new environment varies from one bird to the other. Some of them are very brave and curious while others are a little more nervous. All you have to do is be patient with the bird and let this become an easy transition.

Make sure that everyone in your family follows these rules. If you have children at home, do not allow them to make sudden gestures or even tease the bird. It will only startle him and lengthen his adjustment process. The calmer you are around the bird, the calmer he will be. While it may seem like nothing to us, new sounds and smells are stressful for birds.

2. Introducing him to other pets
If you have pets at home, you naturally want them to get along. However, do not be fooled by videos of birds playing comfortably with dogs or cats. This requires you to either raise them together from a young age or have a bird and another pet that are naturally compatible with one another.

Instinctively, a cat or a dog is a natural predator for your Ringneck. So, the interactions should always be supervised to avoid untoward incidents. The first step is to introduce them while the bird is in the cage.

This should only be done when the bird is comfortably settled in your house. Place the cage in a room that the dog or cat usually rests in. Make sure that both of them are calm during the introduction. If you see the bird thrashing around at the sight of the dog or cat or if you see an aggressive response from your pet, try again. They will reach a point where they actually ignore each other's presence.

Then, if you want to introduce them without any barrier, you could try, but this must only be done when you are comfortable handling the bird. Should there be an ugly scene, you should be able to get the bird away immediately.

Animals and birds are curious by nature. No matter how gentle your pet is, remember that he will always hold the place of a predator. Even a curious lick by a dog or cat can be dangerous, as the saliva of other animals, especially cats, is toxic to the bird.

That said, interactions, however peaceful, should be monitored. The sheer difference in size is a hazard to your bird. Even if the dog just gently nips at the bird, it could prove to be fatal.

While everyone dreams of having pets that can play with each other, irrespective of species, always be on guard. The dog or cat should never be allowed to climb the cage. This is a big stressor for your bird and can lead to stress-related health issues.

If you are not in the house, keep the bird in the cage securely. It also helps to keep your pet restrained with a leash or in a crate. Even the gentlest pet can be a threat to your bird. If there should be an accident, you cannot hold either of them responsible. Remember, even the Ringneck can injure your pet with his beak and toes. For the safety of both pets, never let them interact without barriers when you are not around.

3. Introducing him to an existing flock

Introducing your Ringeneck to an existing flock is not as simple as just putting him in the cage with other birds. You have to take a lot of precautionary measures to ensure that these interactions are peaceful and free from any aggressive response.

The first and most important thing is to quarantine your new bird. He should be kept in a separate room entirely for at least 30 days. This will allow you to check for any health issues. Even if the bird is a carrier, you will be able to prevent any disease spreading throughout the flock with proper quarantining measures.

When you have quarantined the bird, make sure that you do not interact with the other birds after you have interacted with him. This means that the existing flock should be fed and cleaned first. If you must interact with the existing flock after you have spent time with the quarantined bird, make sure that you wash your hands thoroughly.

Introduce the birds one after the other after the quarantine period is over. Start with the bird that is calmest of the lot. Place him and the new bird in separate carriers, next to each other. You can let them out and observe the behavior when you are around to supervise.

If there is an aggressive response, try again. If not, put the birds back in and then keep them with each other for a few days. Repeat this with all the birds in the cage so they are familiar with each other.

Once this is done, put the birds in the cage together and let them be. Unless you see any aggressive behavior, you can let the birds be. Small squabbles are natural, as the flock is simply establishing a pecking order among them.

Remember that with Ringnecks, making introductions during the bluffing phase is not a good idea. It will lead to some nasty fights. Younger birds are easiest to introduce to the flock, as they will not be perceived as a threat.

4. Bonding with the bird

The more time you can spend with your bird, the better. Understand how your bird responds and also learn to communicate with him to make your bond with your bird stronger.

Reading his body language

The bird uses his whole body to show you different emotions. The more you interact with the bird, the more you will become aware of subtle signs that the bird will show. There are a few basic signs, however, that will help you begin your communication with your bird and read his response correctly.

Eyes

- The eyes of the bird will dilate depending upon the level of excitement, curiosity, anger or fear. This is called pinning or flashing.
- Make sure that you take the context of the environment around your bird and his general body posture to understand exactly what the bird is trying to communicate with his eyes.

Wings

- The bird will flap his wings as a form of exercise in most cases.

- Flapping the wings is also a way to get your attention simply because your bird is happy to see you.
- Flapping the wing can be a sign of pain or anger. If you cannot see any stimulus for either, then the bird is probably just fluffing up his feathers.
- Drooping wings are a sign of fatigue. If the wings droop even when the bird is resting, it is a sign that your bird is unwell.

Tail
- Like any other animal, the tail is an important medium of communication.
- Wagging the tail indicates that your bird is happy.
- If he fans out his tail feathers, the bird is trying to show dominance by looking larger. This is done during the breeding season or just before he is going to attack.
- Bobbing of the tail after play and exercise indicates that the bird is just trying to catch his breath.
- Bobbing of the tail otherwise is an indication of respiratory issues.

Leg and feet
- Tapping the feet is often seen as a sign of aggression in your bird. He does this to assert dominance.
- The legs will appear weak after you have played with your bird and are putting him back in the cage. This is no cause for worry as the bird is just resisting going back in to the cage.

Beak
- Grinding of the beak shows that your bird is happy and content.
- If he clicks the beak once, he is simply greeting you and saying hello.
- Multiple clicks on the other hand are a warning signs and it is best that you stay away from your bird.

Body posture
- If the body of the bird is erect and alert but the muscles are relaxed, it shows that he is happy.
- An alert body with stiff muscles means that the bird is showing dominance and is probably going to attack.

Vocalization
- Sounds like chattering, whistling and singing are a song of contentment in your bird.
- Growling and purring indicates aggression or disapproval.
- Clicking of the tongue means that he wants to play with you.

These signs will become clearer as you interact with your bird. You will also see certain movements and body postures unique to your bird and it will help you understand what he exactly wants.

Training your Ringneck parrot
Ringneck parrots are highly intelligent birds. They respond to training positively and can learn a lot of new tricks. Training your Ringneck is not only a great way to bond with him but will also keep him mentally active.

There are some basic things that you must teach your parrot to make sure that they are comfortable being handled as well. The only rule with parrot training is to stay consistent and to shower him with positive reinforcement to make him respond better.

Step up training
Teaching your parrot to step up on your finger or on a perch makes him more hand tamed. Besides that, a bird that will willingly step up is easier to rescue from an unsavory situation such as a fight with a household pet or even an accident such as a fire in the house. Here are a few simple steps to begin step up training with your bird:

- If your bird is hand tamed, you can expect him to step up right away. If not, you have to first make him comfortable enough to approach your hand.

- Holding a treat through the cage bars is the first step. Then you can work your way towards him, opening the door and using the treat to lure the bird out of the cage.

- When the bird is comfortable with approaching you, you can hold out your finger like a perch or use an actual one.

- Then, hold a treat just behind the perch or your finger and wait for the bird to step up voluntarily before handing it out to him. Use the cue "Up" or "Step up" every time you do so.

- Do not be surprised if the bird tries to get his beak around your finger. He is only making sure that the perch is steady. Withdrawing the hand sharply will make him lose trust.

- Once the bird has stepped up, offer the treat and then set him back in the cage with another treat or toy.

- You can slowly try to hold him on the finger or perch and get him out of the cage and walk around for a while. Remember, when you put him back, make it a positive experience by providing treats.

- You can do the same to get him to step up on your shoulder or head once he is comfortable.

- Eventually, the bird will respond to the cue and will not require a treat in order to step up.

Potty training your bird

Just like you potty train your dog or cat, you can teach your Ringneck to "go" in a certain place. This will need you to observe how frequently he poops and be ready before he does.

- When the bird is about to poop, he will show some changes in his body language. Most often, the bird will lift his tail and will seem to push his body weight towards his vent. It will almost look like he is going to squat.

- Then, place a piece of paper below the bird and wait for him to poop. When he does so, shower him with appreciation and give him his favorite treat.

- Soon the bird will associate the piece of paper as the appropriate place to go.

- Even when the bird is out of the cage and you see him getting into the pooping position, just hold the paper out.

- With practice, your bird will look for the paper to poop on.

- Of course, there will be several accidents until your bird figures this out, be patient and let him learn what is expected from him.

Training your bird to talk
The best thing about Indian Ringnecks is their ability to mimic human voice and words. They will also pick up on regular sounds around your home such as the doorbell. You can teach them the words that you want by repeating them constantly.

- If you want your parrot to mimic your words, you need to spend time talking to them. To begin with, start with a few words. Say hello and bye every time you see the bird or leave the room.

- You can even leave on shows like cartoon that have high-pitched voices so your bird can pick up on them.

- When you are teaching your bird a certain word, repeat it to him in a slow and high-pitched manner.

- Soon, you will see him mumbling to himself. This is him practicing what you say to him.

- Before you know it, your "Hello" will be returned with another by the bird.

- Ringnecks pick up on words even when you do not intend to teach them a certain word, so be careful about what you say in front of your bird.

5. Feeding your bird

The diet that you provide your bird should be well balanced and should contain a good balance of fresh and dry foods. Most health and behavioral issues in birds are related to nutritional deficiencies. This can be averted by making sure that you give your bird a good routine and diet.

Seeds

Seeds should be a part of your bird's diet, as they are included in their natural diet. Many breeders will tell you that seeds are bad for your bird. This is when the bird relies solely on seeds for nutrition. When you give the bird seeds in moderation, he will get an adequate supply of fats that is necessary for several metabolic functions.

Seeds and pellets

It is not a good idea to mix pellets with seeds. Pellets are usually fortified with several vitamins and are great for your bird. However, mixing pellets and seeds will make your bird only pick the seed and leave the pellets out. It is a better idea to distribute them through the week. You can provide them with pellets three times a week and seeds four times a week or vice versa.

Sometimes the bird may refuse to eat pellets. Then you can introduce pellets in small portions with the seeds and keep increasing the quantity until it is fully replaced by pellets.

Fruits and vegetables

Fruits are essential to the bird's diet. Fruits with a lot of pulp and texture work best for these birds. Your options include apples, grapes, kiwis, pears and mangos. The fruits can be warmed slightly to make it easy for the bird to digest them. If the fruit stays uneaten for a few hours, make sure that you take it out of the bowl before it spoils.

In addition to fruits, vegetables are also essential. There are several vegetables like carrots, leafy greens, pumpkin squash, banana squash, zucchini and others. If you can cube and cook the larger vegetables, the bird enjoys it more.

The good thing with fruits and vegetables is that you can give your bird a large variety of options to choose from.

Protein

Ringnecks need a certain amount of proteins. You can provide the bird with shredded chicken, cooked meat or even boiled eggs. Offer protein once a week to make sure that the balance is maintained.

With Ringnecks, feeding them is not very hard. They are willing to eat just about anything. Make sure that you do not include any oil, sugar, salt or preservatives to keep your bird healthy.

6. Grooming your bird

Grooming your Indian Ringneck is not very difficult. They will preen themselves, will take a bath in a water bowl that is placed in the cage and will keep themselves clean for the most part. However, a few grooming sessions with your bird will help build a strong bond between you and your bird.

Bathing your bird

Indian Ringnecks love to take a bath, so this should not require a lot of effort from your end. The only time you will have to give your bird a good scrub is if he gets any debris on his feathers or if he has some toxic material like paint on his feathers.

To urge your bird to get into a water bath, you can place a few spinach leaves or other greens in the water bath. When he steps into the bath, he will not only enjoy a good bath but will also have treats to go with it.

If the bird is hand tamed, you can pick him up and lower him into the water bowl, feet first. Slowly let him in and then allow him to enjoy the water.

The water should be lukewarm. Soap will only be used when there is some rigid dirt on the feather. Use diluted baby soap and gently brush the debris off with a toothbrush. Rinse it thoroughly and make sure that there is no chemical residue on the body of the bird.

Misting the feathers with a spray bottle also helps keep your bird clean. If he resists, you should stop immediately. Never spray on the face and eyes directly. It will be very uncomfortable for the bird to get any water in the nostrils and eyes.

Trimming the nails

If the nails of your bird grow too long, they will get caught in upholstery threads or in rope toys. If the bird tries to move, there are chances that he could break the nail, or worse, fracture the toe. This can be very painful, which is why trimming the nails is necessary.

Textured perches are the best option when it comes to keeping the nails trimmed naturally. If you still see that the nail is overgrown, it should be trimmed. A very sharp end on the toenail means that it requires trimming.

To trim the nail of the bird, wrap a towel around him and hold him on your lap on his stomach. Then release one foot from under the towel. Place your finger under the toenail and gently file the nail until it does not feel sharp anymore. Repeat this on the other side to make sure that the nails are filed properly.

If your bird resists, take it easy, as the toes are very delicate. You can trim one toe, let the bird rest and then move on to the next one. Make sure that the nail is not so short that it hampers the bird's ability to perch and climb.

Clipping the nail

You can clip the nails and still allow the bird to fly close to the ground. Many bird owners are not comfortable with this and if you believe that it may hamper the safety of your bird, you need to take adequate measures.

Clipping the tail can be tricky. You need to make sure that you do not get the blood feathers of the bird, which can cause profuse bleeding. The primary feathers are the ones that need to be clipped. These are the three largest feathers on the wings of the bird.

Cutting about 1 cm is good enough to prevent the bird from getting a very good lift for flight. Hold the bird with a towel wrapped around him. Rest him on your thigh, face down. Then spread the feathers of one wing out while keeping the other wing under the towel.

Using a sharp pair of scissors, cut up to 1 cm off the primary feathers. Do the same on the other side, making sure that they are symmetrical. When they are not symmetrical, the bird will find it hard to maintain balance and will be unable to even stay on the perch comfortably.

Even when the bird's wings have been clipped, they should not be left outdoors without any restraint such as a leash or a carrier. If there is a breeze that is strong enough to give him the lift he needs, he can get away.

7. Finding an avian vet

This is the most crucial part in providing good care for your bird. With birds, you will require someone who specializes in treating health issues specific to them. While your local vet can be very helpful in treating emergencies, you will require a specialized avian vet to help you maintain the health of your Indian Ringneck.

An avian vet has dedicated his or her practice to treating exotic birds and understanding their anatomy. While their educational qualification is the same as a vet who works with pets like dogs or cat, the practice involves birds.

Avian vets are often part of authorized organizations like the Association of Avian Vets. This helps them stay updated and learn about the new techniques of treating health issues related to birds.

If you are a new parrot owner, your avian vet will be a reliable source of information for you.

Locating your avian vet

The most difficult part about having a pet bird is locating a qualified avian vet. There are a few resources that you can try to find good leads:

- The yellow pages is the best way to start. This will have a list of specialized vets along with their qualifications.

- The official website of the Association of Avian vets will list a number of qualified avian vets who will be able to care for your bird.
- You can contact the veterinary medical association in your state for information.

- Speak to other bird owners and look for reliable vets in your vicinity.

The closer your vet is to your home, the easier it will be to take your bird for a checkup. Additionally, a vet who is located nearby will be able to deal with emergencies more effectively.

What to ask the vet
To be sure that you have chosen the right vet to treat your bird, here are a few questions that you should ask him or her upon your first visit:

- **How long have they been working with birds?** The more experience they have, the better qualified they are. You need to find someone who has a solid background to make sure that your beloved pet is in good hands.

- **Have you worked with Ringnecks before?** Although it may seem like all parrots are the same, each species has its own requirements and demands. The more your vet has worked with the species of parrot that you have, the more experience they will have.

- **Are you part of the AAV?** While it doesn't mean that a vet who is not part of this organization is not qualified enough, someone who is part of it is definitely a lot more reassuring. The AAV only promotes the highest quality medical healthcare for birds and ensures that all its members are updated.

- **Do you have birds at home?** It is certainly an advantage if your vet is a bird owner. That will give him or her a lot of hands on experience with the body language of the bird, which will help make treatment sessions less stressful.
- **Is there an after-hours facility or emergency facility?** An accident does not occur with warning, so you need a vet who can be available or make some medical assistance available to your bird should some such incident occur.
- **What are your fees?** This is definitely a question you should ask, even if you feel awkward about it. If you are unable to afford the veterinary charges of a certain vet, you can look for

more options. Every vet will have a fee schedule chart that will tell you what exactly you can expect when you sign up for a service.

- **Are house calls an option?** In some cases, the bird may be too severely injured or unwell to take him to the vet. Then, it will become necessary for the vet to come to you.

- **How many examinations are recommended per year?** Usually, a vet will recommend about one thorough examination per year. This is done to make sure that your bird is always in good health.

A qualified avian vet will answer all your questions patiently and without any hesitation. The manner in which they respond to questions will also tell you if their personality is compatible with you or not. This goes a long way in building a good relationship with your vet.

Other considerations

- Watch how your vet interacts with the bird on the first visit. They must be confident to handle the bird and should be comfortable.

- How does the staff help to make the visit less stressful for the bird? Are they interacting with you in a good manner?

Once you are convinced that a certain vet is perfect for your bird, you will be in partnership with them to provide a healthy life for your bird.

8. Travelling with your bird

If you are moving to a new home that is across state or country borders, you may have to travel with your bird. If you can drive to your new home, then it is much less stressful, as the rules are the same as the ones you followed when you brought your bird home from the breeders.

The real challenge is when you have to travel by air with your bird. Being in the cargo area at such a high altitude can be very stressful for your bird and can even lead to seizures or death when the airline is not responsible.

Before you look for airlines that will let you travel with your bird, you need to make sure that your Ringneck is allowed to enter a certain state or country. There are strict laws with respect to importing exotic parrot species in several parts of the world.

Contacting the Wildlife and Fisheries Authority in the country or state that you are travelling to will help you understand the legal considerations. You can also visit the official website of CITES to understand the laws that apply to your Indian Ringneck when crossing borders.

If there is any paperwork that needs to be done, make sure that you plan at least 6 months in advance. You do not want any delays to cause problems in your travel plans.

If the bird is allowed to enter a state or country, he will require a health certificate. This should be made not more than 30 days before your travel dates.

Then, contact an airline that allows pets on board. You will have to purchase a carrier that is approved by the airline. When you are ready to travel, line the carrier with enough bedding and leave a toy for your bird to have something familiar with him. Water should be provided in bottles to prevent dampness and related infections.

The airline will be able to feed your bird at regular intervals. Of course, there is an additional service charge for this. Make sure that the cage is secured properly and the door is shut tight.

You do not want to have a bird on the loose during the customs check. Once you have reached your new home, treat it like your bird's first day in his old home. Leave him alone and reduce interaction until he is well adjusted.

Having the bird checked within 24 hours of reaching the new home will be beneficial. There could be minor stress-related health issues that can be treated easily. Even if your bird seems perfectly healthy, a good check-up is mandatory.

If you are unable to travel with your bird, you can look for friends and family who can take care of him. There are also several authorized pet-sitting agencies that will be able to help you find a qualified and experienced pet sitter.

There may come a time when you will have to find a new home for your bird. It could be a dream job in a place where your bird cannot go with you or marriage could make you have to move homes. In that case, a rescued bird should be handed over to the shelter he was adopted from. You can alternatively look for a good foster home or a new family who will be able to commit to your bird just like you did.

Chapter 4: Breeding Ringnecks

Indian Ringnecks will become sexually mature between the ages of 2 and 3. Females generally reach sexual maturity earlier than males. If you wish to breed your Indian Ringneck, you need to make sure that you follow the right techniques to ensure a healthy clutch and good quality hatchlings.

1. Finding a suitable pair

If you have a single Ringneck parrot at home, introducing a mate can be tricky. When they are hormonal, females especially, they tend to be territorial and aggressive. She is the one that sets the tone of the courting period. If the birds are left unsupervised, the female can cause severe injuries and can potentially kill the male bird.

You will know that a female Ringneck is ready to mate when you see her spending a lot of time in the nesting box. You must never introduce a male companion immediately. Start by placing the cage of the male bird near the female's cage and allow them to get used to one another.

When the female is adjusted to the presence of her potential mate, she will show signs of being interested in him. To begin with, she will be seen clinging on to the cage bar on the side that is close to the cage of the male bird.

The male will respond by pinning of his eyes and the female will keep her head tilted backwards. Even when they are in this stage, it is advisable to keep them apart. You can do this for about one more week until you are certain that the female is interested in the male bird.

Once she shows genuine interest, you can place the birds together. It is best to put them in a different cage altogether. If not, you must put the female bird in the cage of the male and not vice versa.

This will prevent excessive territorial behavior from the female. Nevertheless, you can expect the female to chase the male bird around in the cage. That is when you need to be extra attentive. If you notice any signs of aggression, it means that you will have to separate them and try again or will have to look for a new mate altogether.

During the introduction, clipping the wings of the female bird is a good idea while keeping the wings of the male intact. That way, the female will have enough flight to reach up to the nesting box. As for the male bird, he will be able to escape any sudden attack.

If you want to pair two birds in particular but are finding it hard to get them to be compatible, you can try by changing the location of the cage or putting them in a new age. When they are introduced in a completely unfamiliar environment, they tend to bond with one another and will also become less aggressive.

Make sure that new interactions are supervised for a few weeks to let the birds become comfortable with one another.

The other option is to house a pair together all year round. This is a better option, as the aggressive behavior is curbed. Since the female has bonded with the male over the year, the chances of her trying to attack him will be highly reduced.

They become more affectionate towards one another and will do everything together throughout the year. Then when the breeding season arrives, they will show more interest in one another.

After this, you can be sure that they will mate and lay their first clutch. Keeping a pair together for a year is a lot more beneficial. You will be able to maintain proper records. You will also be able to predict the types of mutations that may occur with the birds you pair.

2. Hatching and Incubating

Once the pair settles into the nesting box, you can expect the first clutch to be laid anytime.

The eggs of the Ringneck parrot are the size of a quarter and are laid every alternate day until the clutch is complete. The number of eggs in a clutch can vary from 3 to 6 eggs. The eggs are white in color.

One interesting thing about parrots is that the eggs are white in color so that the parent birds can locate them easily in the wild. You see, in their natural habitat, parrots choose dark areas like cavities of trees to nest. The white eggs are easily visible.

On average, a pair of Indian Ringneck parrots will produce two clutches every year. It is also possible for them to lay up to three clutches. For the bird to lay three clutches, you will have to remove the eggs from the nest as soon as the clutch is complete.

If you do practice this, make sure that your birds get additional calcium supplements in the form of leafy vegetables or mineral blocks to help them get enough nutrition.

It is best to allow the mother to incubate the eggs. In case you find that she is unable to do so because of behavioral or health issues, you can place your parrot eggs in an artificial incubator.

You will be able to find incubators at pet stores and also online. The settings can be adjusted as per the species of the bird. Make sure that you turn the eggs as suggested by the manufacturer.

Usually, the incubation of Ringneck parrot eggs takes about 23 days. When the female is incubating her eggs, she will spend most of her time sitting on the eggs. She will only leave the nest to eat and to stretch her wings out every once in a while.

The mother bird will also turn the eggs to ensure that the development of the embryo is even. This also prevents issues like the embryo sticking to one side of the shell.

Just about 2 days before the eggs hatch, the chick will begin to poke a hole from inside. With this hole, the bird gets access to more oxygen, starting the hatching process.

If the weather conditions in the state or city that you live in tend to be dry, having a spray bottle with clean water handy is a good idea. Spray some water inside the nesting box to make the hatching process more comfortable for the baby bird.

The hatching process begins after a hatching ring has been made around the egg. This should take about 15 minutes. After this ring has been made, the chick will maneuver himself out of the egg.

He will break the egg into two sections using his legs. Once the chick has pushed himself out of the egg, the mother bird will remove the egg shells. In case she fails to do so, you can do it yourself to prevent the shell from covering other eggs and leading to complications when they begin to hatch.

3. Raising the chicks

Hand raised chicks are certainly tamer, but if you do not really need a very tame chick, co-parenting with your Ringneck parrot is a good idea. You can provide one meal while the parents provide the others. You can work your way up by increasing the number of feeds you give the baby birds.

You may have to hand raise the baby entirely if the eggs have been hatched in an incubator or if the mother abandons the nest. This will require some commitment and a lot of patience.

You will have to feed the baby birds every two hours, even at night, so you need to be entirely sure that you can continue to do so before you take up this responsibility.

In case you are unable to hand feed the bird or if you think that it is too much work, you can contact your avian vet. There are also several breeders who will be able to foster the chicks.

Ideally, the mother bird should provide for her babies. This will allow the mother to transfer certain nutrients into the baby's body that will help develop a strong immune system.

What you need to know about hand feeding

- It is a tedious task. Newborn chicks are difficult to handle, as they will move around a lot and will get away from you in a jiffy.

- The delicate frame of the bird's body can also be very intimidating to handle.

- Make sure your hands are properly disinfected before you can handle the baby bird.

- If the eggs have been hatched in an incubator, do not feed the bird for up to 6 hours after hatching. If you feed the baby too early, it could be fatal.

- If you are co-parenting the bird, you must first place it in a brooder with an internal temperature of 95 degree Fahrenheit. When the baby is warmed up, you can feed him. If you feel like he is panting or showing discomfort, reduce the temperature.

- When the baby is warm enough, you can feed him. In case the crop is already full with the food provided by the parent birds, wait for it to empty. If food is present in the crop, a milky fluid is seen in the area.

- A syringe or an eyedropper is ideal to feed the baby birds.

Handfeeding tips for one day old Ringneck chicks:
- The food must be warm and should be about 105-108 degrees Fahrenheit in temperature.

- If it is the first feed of the bird, using only an electrolyte solution is recommended.

- The feeding utensils should be cleaned thoroughly.

- The baby should be kept warm at all times. If the body becomes too cool, the digestion process is hampered.

- The bedding in the brooder should be changed every time you feed your baby bird.

- If there is any abnormality, contact your avian vet immediately.

- If your chick is refusing to eat, do not force him.

- The crop should never be over filled, as it can lead to issues like sour crop.

- A couple of drops should be good enough during the bird's first few feeds.

- The bird should be fed every two hours or just before the crop is fully empty.

The first feed

The bird must be handled very gently to make sure that you do not startle or injure the baby bird. Here are a few important guidelines to make the first feeding session less stressful.

- It is recommended that you use some electrolyte solution such as pedialyte that is not flavored.

- The purpose of the electrolyte solution is to make sure that the digestive abilities of the bird are fine.

- When he has emptied the crop, he is ready for the commercially prepared bird formula.

- To give the bird electrolyte, place a small drop on the left side of the bird's mouth. On most cases, the baby will lap it up immediately.

- In case the baby does not show any interest in the food, you have the option of letting him rest for some time and then trying again.

- Some baby chicks will have to practice before they are able to understand how to take in handfed food.

- If after several attempts, your baby bird is not taking any food in, it is possible that the food is not warm enough.

- Dipping the syringe or ink dropper in a glass of warm water before feeding the bird is the best way to keep it warm enough.

4. Weaning

You can wean a baby bird when he is about 4 weeks old. Weaning means to make the bird capable of eating his food without any assistance.

This will take some understanding and training for your baby bird, so you need to be as patient as possible.

Begin by leaving cubes of fresh fruits on the floor of the cage and let the bird inspect it. Since Ringnecks are curious by nature, they will peck at it and try to understand the new food.

They may just leave the food alone and walk away or may try to take a piece off. Let the bird explore and after one hour of providing fresh fruits and vegetables, the cage should be cleaned out to prevent the chances of spoiling foods lying around the cage.

As the bird gets familiar with the new food, he will eat bits of it. Take a note of the types of fruits and vegetables that your bird seems to like and include them in the diet.

Soon, you will see that the bird will begin to lose interest in the formula, as he will be full with the food that he has eaten by himself. You can even try to leave pellets and seeds in the water bowl. As the quantity of eating foods on their own increases, the need for assistance will decrease. That way you will have a bird that has been weaned correctly.

Chapter 5: Health Issues in Indian Ringnecks

Like all birds, Indian Ringneck parrots are susceptible to several infections that can lead to serious health issues. Making sure you give them good food, keep their cage in good condition and also take them for regular visits to the vet will ensure that they are healthier and will have a longer life. This chapter will tell you everything that you need to know about your parrot's health.

1. Identifying illness in birds

With Ringneck parrots, the biggest issue is identifying illnesses at an early stage to make sure that the bird gets the care that he needs. Now, like any other parrot, they are great at concealing the symptoms, allowing the disease to become more intense. However, there are some very subtle signs that you will have to watch out for.

The more you interact with your bird, the more familiar you will become with these signs. That way, you can get them medical attention immediately and avert an unfavorable situation.

Hiding an illness is a part of the bird's instinct to survive. If a predator is able to identify a sick bird, he will become easy prey. That is why birds pretend to be absolutely in good health for as long as they can.

The most common signs of illness in Ringnecks are:

- **The feathers:** A bird who is healthy will have bright eyes and will look perfectly preened. The feathers are held close to the body. On the other hand, a bird that is unwell will keep his feathers puffed up and ruffled for long hours.

  The feathers will also be maintained poorly, as the bird is too unwell to preen. The feathers will appear tattered, dirty and matted. The feather in the vent area should be especially clean. If you see that there are feces stuck on these feathers, it indicates some digestive issue.

- **Posture:** When the bird is perched, he should be upright with the weight distributed evenly on the feet. The tip of the wing should cross over at the back and the tail feathers should remain straight.

  If you notice drooping wings with the tail drawn inwards, it shows some discomfort. In addition to this, any low posture or wobbly stance on the perch is an indication of abnormality. Any indication of constant weight shift and restlessness is a sign of injury or any dysfunction in the feet because of a disease. In some cases, this can be an indication of tumors in the kidney.

- **Attitude:** The bird will show behavioral changes when he is sick. You will notice that the level of activity decreases. The bird will also vocalize a lot less when he is unwell. There may be drastic changes in personality. For instance, a friendly bird might suddenly become irritable and aggressive or a bird that is normally aggressive is suddenly very easy to handle. Either way, you have some abnormality in the bird.

- **The beak:** In birds, the beak is growing constantly. This is because normal activity leads to some wear and tear that needs to be repaired. If you notice that the beak is growing too fast or if you see that the quality of the beak is deteriorating, then the bird may have developed health issues.

  For instance, when the bird has any liver disease, you will notice black spots on the beak with an overgrowth. So, an abnormal rate of growth should not be taken lightly. Look for any crust or enlargement in the mouth and the beak of the bird.

- **The feet:** No matter how many precautions you take, birds tend to develop infections in the feet. There are pressure sores that develop when the perch is improper. Some of the most common issues that you will see in the feet are soreness, lameness, swelling, redness and constant weight shift.

  If any of these problems are associated with the leg band, make sure it is removed immediately. If there is any flakiness or crustiness on the feet, it is a sign of a parasitic infection or any nutritional deficiency.

- **The respiratory tract:** In healthy birds, breathing is very comfortable and does not require any effort. If the bird continues to breathe heavily even when he is at rest, it is an indication of some issue. There must not be any noises when the bird is breathing. Sounds like wheezing, clicking or sneezing are an indication of illness in the bird.

  You will also notice nasal discharge in the bird with some staining on the feathers covering the area just above the nostril. Pink eye or conjunctivitis is also common when there are respiratory issues. This leads to redness and swelling along with some discharge near the eyes.

  A bird that is finding it hard to breathe is easy to recognize. The mouth will remain open and the bird will actually gasp for breath. Besides infections in the respiratory tract, labored breathing is also the result of abdominal infections.

  You will see the bird bob his tail up and down, showing that there is some enlargement in the abdomen or some form of respiratory tract infection. Heart disease can also be indicated by labored breathing.

- **Consumption of food:** The bird will be unable to eat well when he is sick. With the rate of metabolism that is prevalent in their bodies, this can be a serious issue.

  You need to keep an eye on the food consumed by your bird on a daily basis. The seeds when eaten are hulled and then swallowed. On the other hand, the bird will just pick up the seed and drop it on the floor when he is not interested.

  At times, the bird may eat the seed without hulling, leaving hulled seeds on the floor of the cage. This can also be caused when the bird is vomiting or regurgitating.

Regurgitation is common in Ringnecks, as it is a type of courtship behavior. If the bird has been vomiting, you will see that the ejected food will stick to the floor and the bars of the cage.

- **Consumption of water:** Although it may seem like the bird does not drink too much water, it is necessary to make sure that he gets enough clean water to drink. Whether the bird drinks too much water or very little water, it is a sign of some metabolic issue or an issue related to the digestive tract of the bird. Just keep tabs on how much water is left in the bowl when you clean it out everyday. If it is more or less than usual, contact your vet to be entirely sure.

- **Droppings:** One of the best indicators of health is the dropping of the bird. If you see that the frequency reduces or increases, keep an eye on the bird. If reduced food intake is the reason for reduced droppings, talk to your vet.

  It is true that the droppings will change color when different foods are consumed. However, if you notice abnormal coloration, it can indicate health problems in the bird. If the consistency of the dropping changes, it can also be an indication of digestive issues or other health disorders. Cleaning the bedding and substrate regularly will help you keep an eye on the droppings.

  Any signs of blood in the droppings is certainly a red flag. There are several issues related to the cloaca, the oviduct and the digestive tract that lead to this. It can also be a warning sign for a tumor that is developing on the body of the bird.

- **Unusual growth on the body:** Cysts on the feathers, abscesses or any swelling on the body must be reported to the vet. The bird must not have any fat deposit on the abdomen and the chest. If you see any enlargement in the body, it could be a sign of tumor. Handling your bird regularly and keeping an eye on these issues will help you seek help at early stages of the disease. The more you interact with your bird, the easier it is to detect any growth or abnormality on his body.

Now that you have a fair idea about how different symptoms manifest, the only thing that you need to do is keep an eye on your bird. Inspect the cage regularly and also handle your bird as frequently as you can.

Annual examinations that include a fecal analysis and blood tests are highly recommended. They can help you detect any abnormality at the earliest. That way the chances of recovery from any illness are also high.

If you do have a few false alarms once in a while, it does not mean that you are overprotective. The more cautious you are, the healthier your bird will be.

2. Common diseases affecting Ringnecks
There are certain diseases that Ringnecks are most susceptible to. It could be because they act as hosts for certain parasites and also because they are genetically inclined to certain health issues. This section lists out the major health issues that you need to watch out for when you bring home an Indian Ringneck:

Polyoma
This disease normally affects birds that are younger, most often just when they are born. Adults will develop immunity to this disease over time.

The disease is caused by a virus called the Polyoma Virus.

Symptoms:
- There are very few external symptoms for this condition.

- The bird will die suddenly within 48 hours of contracting the disease, often with no symptoms at all.

Remedies:
- Make sure that the birds are vaccinated as soon as they are born.

- Preventive care is the best way to make sure that your bird is safe.

- Adopt proper quarantine practices.

- Make sure that people who have been in contact with other birds wash their hands and feet completely before you allow them to interact with your bird.

- Maintain a hygienic environment for your bird to live in.

Beak and feather syndrome

This condition is also known as Psittacine Beak and Feather Disease and mostly affects Cockatoos. However, several cases of Ringnecks developing the condition have been reported. This condition affects older birds in most cases.

Symptoms:
- The feathers seem to be gnarled and swollen.

- New feathers that develop after molting will look abnormal.

- The beak will look dull and dusty,f as it is covered with feather dust.

- The development of the beak is abnormal.

- In extreme cases, it can also lead to paralysis in the bird.

Treatment:
- There is no treatment for PBFD and the bird will either die or will become a carrier.

- It is best to isolate any bird that is infected.
- Sometimes, when the condition is very severe, euthanizing is the only option.

- Since the condition is usually spread by feces and feather dander, proper hygiene can help control the condition.

Proventricular Dilation Disease

Also known as Macaw Wasting Disease, this condition is common in all parrot breeds. It is highly contagious but stays dormant for several years. Therefore, it is a very difficult disease to diagnose.

Symptoms:
- Seizures
- Heart attacks
- Tremors
- Paralysis
- Lack of coordination

Treatment:
- There is no medication that is known to treat this condition yet.

- Make sure that you include digestible supplements in the diet of your bird after consulting an avian vet.

- Changing the diet of the bird is also useful in prolonging his life.

Papilloma

This condition will most often affect the vent area of the bird and in some cases, the throat and the mouth. While the disease in itself is not fatal, the papilloma can choke the bird when it develops in the throat and mouth.

Symptoms:
- Wart-like growth in the vent area or in the throat and mouth.

- Changed behavior in the bird

- Labored breathing due to blocked respiratory tract

Treatment:
- Laser surgery to remove the growth.

- Surgical removal of this growth.

Psittacosis
This condition is commonly known as parrot fever and is a disease that can affect a bird at any age. It is caused by a highly potent bacteria that belongs to the same strain that causes chlamydosis in pet birds.

Symptoms:
- Nasal discharge
- Sneezing
- Sinusitis
- Conjunctivitis
- Pneumonia
- Lime green colored droppings
- Seizures
- Tremors
- Paralysis
- Death

Treatment:
- Tetracycline drugs are administered.

- The most recommended medicine today is doxycycline.

- The medication is normally administered through the drinking water, but if the bird does not drink medicated water, they can be injected too.

- The cage and aviary must be cleaned and disinfected after treatment.

- Preventive measures are a must, as this can lead to Chlamydia in people.

E-coli infection
E-coli bacteria is part of the flora of the body of parrots. This means that the microorganism lives in the digestive tract of your Ringneck parrot and actually benefits the bodily functions.

However, disease and untimely death are possible when the bacteria enters the reproductive system, the respiratory system or the bloodstream of the bird.

Symptoms:
- Culturing the bacteria and testing them for antibiotic susceptibility is the first step.

- It benefits to understand if the bacteria are causing a certain disease of if your bird is experiencing some form of secondary infection.

- Coliform infections are common in the respiratory system and that is when it could be fatal.

- Keeping the bird's environment clean goes a long way in preventing this condition.

- Keep the inside and the outside of the cage as clean as possible.

Gout
Gout is the result of calcification in the kidneys. Young birds that do not receive a proper balance of calcium in the diet can be susceptible. This is a disease which is primarily diet related.

The formula that you give the baby bird should be suitable to its metabolism to prevent gout.

Symptoms:
- The initial symptoms are very mild.

- Regurgitation of the food and dehydration occurs in the initial stages.

- The baby bird looks smaller than usual.

- High concentration of urates are revealed with blood tests.

- The skin on the chest looks wrinkled.

- The bird is unable to retain anything including fluids in the crop.

- When the symptoms become obvious, your bird is possibly close to the end of its life.

Treatment:
- Keep the baby bird well hydrated.

- Probenecid or Colochicine is administered to keep the heart safe.

- Urates can be removed from the bloodstream with Allopurinal.

Aspergillosis
This airborne disease affects the lungs of the bird. It is caused by a fungal infection due to improper cage sanitation. If the food is damp and spoilt, it will become a harboring site for the fungi. In addition to that, cage grates and food or water bowls with fecal deposits will lead to fungal infections.

Low humidity and dust in the environment also lead to this infection.

Symptoms:
- Lack of appetite
- Reduced or excessive consumption of water
- Change in the voice
- Depression
- Excessive urination
- Lethargy
- Change in the behavior
- Paralysis
- Ataxia or loss of muscle control

Treatment:
- Inrtacocozole and Fluconozole are administered.

- Keeping the environment of the bird clean is a preventive measure.

- Make sure that you only give your bird clean and fresh food and water.

Salmonellosis
This is a very serious bacterial infection in birds. It can also be passed on to humans. With parrots, the mortality rate is very high and it also leads to many carriers if even one bird in your flock is infected. In the acute stage, the condition is normally treated with antibiotics. However, for most part, the birds will not show any symptoms.

Treatment:
- The fecal culture of newborn birds should be screened. This helps reveal if a bird is shedding.

- Infected birds should never be bred.

- If you want to breed the bird, make sure that it is isolated with its partner and that all the eggs are artificially incubated.

Sinusitis
The exact cause of the condition remains unknown. It is one disease that is quite complex and can be highly contagious. Respiratory problems such as breathlessness and labored breathing are associated with his condition.

Treatment:
- If the causal factor is a secondary infection, it is a little more complex to treat.

- Providing vitamin A supplement has proved useful in most cases.

Proteus and pseudomonas infection

This infection can affect the eyes, the digestive system and the upper and lower respiratory system among other organs. This condition is caused when the bird consumes spoilt food. Poor hygiene also leads to infections.

Treatment:

- Antibiotic susceptibility tests on the culture are needed to develop a long term treatment process.

- Pseudomonas is resistant to most antibiotics.

Molting

This is a very stressful condition for your bird. This is when the old feathers are shed and new feathers grow in their place.

You will notice that your bird is less active and is very irritable. A keratin cuticle that appears like a waxy layer is removed as the bird preens itself. After the new feathers have grown, the bird spends a lot of time preening and almost appears like he is scratching himself all the time.

There are also chances that you will notice pieces of this cuticle on the body of the bird. It is very easy to mistake this for feather dander.

Treatment:

- The bird should not have any stressors in his environment.

- A balanced diet with vitamin supplements is necessary.

- You can mist the body of the bird regularly to make the irritation lesser.

- It also helps to give the bird baths frequently.

- You can also make sure that your bird gets enough rest.

- If, in the process of preening, the bird is damaging his own feathers, you must contact your vet immediately. This could indicate behavioral issues like feather plucking.

The most vital thing with Ringneck health is to maintain a clean environment and to provide good food. There must not be any room for the pathogens to thrive if you want to make sure that your bird is safe at all times. Regular vet checkups will help detect any disease at an early stage and thus provide better options to treat the condition.

3. Behavioral issues in Ringnecks

Studies reveal that Ringneck parrots are highly intelligent and a lot more intelligent than the pets that we commonly have in our homes. In addition to that, they also have a very long life. These are the two primary causes for several behavioral issues in parrots.

It is very easy for them to figure out ways to manipulate their owners and thus develop behavioral issues. For example, if you pay attention to your bird when he screams, even if it means that you are asking him to stop, he will learn that this will shift your focus on him.

Boredom is the number one cause for all behavioral issues in birds including feather plucking. They also tend to mutilate their own skin in the process. It is mandatory for you to understand how you can keep your bird entertained enough so that he does not develop these issues.

If the diet of the bird is not good enough and he lives on a poor diet for several years on end, behavioral problems can also develop due to poor nutrition. This is why vets recommend that you ensure that you have enough knowledge about birds before you bring one home.

The common behavioral issues with parrots are:

Chewing

While chewing is a natural behavior for birds, it can become a problem when chewing is directed at your valuable belongings. In the wild, a parrot will chew on branches and twigs to make his nest or home "customized".

Chewing is also very important for the bird to maintain his beak and keep it sharp. However, when it is not supervised and directed correctly, chewing can even become hazardous. For instance, a bird can chew on electric wires and get electrocuted or even start an electrical fire.

It is necessary for you to "parrot proof" your home to make it safe for the bird and also to keep your valuables out of the way. You can bring your bird several toys that they are allowed to chew on. This includes cuttlebones, branches, hard toys and lots more. Keep rotating these toys over the weeks to ensure that your bird remains interested in them.

Also make sure that your bird is always supervised when he is out of the cage. There is always a chance of accidents when you fail to do so.

Biting

The manner in which you approach your bird is very important. If you have any feelings of stress, anxiety or nervousness, your bird will catch on immediately. Any apprehension when you approach the bird leads to a defensive bite. Remember, birds don't think much; they react to the stimulus that they get.

Another common cause for biting is using your hands to punish the bird. If you shoo the bird with a sharp wave or perhaps toss things at the bird, a negative association is created immediately.

What you can do is help your bird associate the hand with positive things. Hand feeding or giving the bird treats with your hand tells them that they have nothing to worry about when you approach them.

Lastly, territorial behavior makes the bird nippy. This happens especially when they are nesting or in their breeding season. Females tend to be more hormonal and territorial.

There are some things that you can do when the bird bites in order to correct the behavior:

- When the bird is about to bite, blow on his face gently to distract him.

- If your bird is perched on your arm when he is about to bite, just drop your hand by a few inches. This will put the bird out of balance, and any bird hates an unsteady perch. He will immediately learn that biting makes him lose balance.

- Just put the bird down on the floor if he bites. They are not happy being on the ground, as it makes them feel vulnerable and will immediately distract them.

The one thing that you should never do is scream or shout at the bird. This is a response to the bird's behavior and that is precisely what he is looking for.

Training your bird to step up and to make him associate your hands with positive things is a sure shot way of keeping your bird's biting behavior at bay.

Screaming
Vocalizing at a certain time of the day, particularly at dawn and dusk, is common for Ringnecks. The only time you have an issue is when the screaming is a result of your going away from your bird or the bird not getting his way.

The best way to prevent screaming in Ringnecks is to make sure that you ignore the bird completely. That means you must not even look at the bird. Yelling at the bird and asking him to stop only reinforces the behavior.

Then, reward the bird when he behaves appropriately. For example, if the bird begins to scream when you leave the room, let him do so. The moment he stops screaming and you can count up to 5 or 10, reward him.

You can also look for specific triggers that are making your bird scream. If it is something that threatens the bird, for instance a large bright object, just get it out of his sight to calm him down.

Ignoring the screaming bird is a habit that everyone in your family must practice. You need to make sure that no one responds to the bird with any sound or eye contact.

Redirecting your bird with foraging toys before you leave the room is one way of calming him down when screaming is associated with separation anxiety.

Phobia or anxiety

The first thing that you need to understand is the difference between phobia and fear. Fear is a good thing as long as it is rational. This includes your bird being wary of new people, new toys or a new environment. This can be reversed by familiarizing the bird with the change.

On the other hand, phobia is the excessive and irrational need to get away from a particular situation, object or person. You know that your bird is phobic when he will do anything he can to get away from his object of terror. This includes:

- Running
- Pushing his head through the cage bars, sometimes until he bleeds
- Crashing into walls violently
- Resisting strongly
- Aggressive response such as biting
- Throwing himself on the back to appear dead
- Fear of coming out of the cage
- Self-mutilation
- Feather plucking.

You will mostly find phobias in birds that have been rescued from long-term abuse and neglect. Improper breeding practices that do not allow the chick to develop properly can also lead to phobias. If the bird is force-weaned, the emotional development of the bird is stunted, leading to irrational fears.

There are several other factors such as a lack of socialization, being separated from other chicks in the flock too early, clipping the wings improperly or any traumatic injury or accident will lead to phobia in your bird.

That said, some birds are also genetically predisposed to being more anxious. You can seek your vet's assistance to provide medication to your bird to calm him down and reduce anxiety if you notice that it is affecting the well being of your bird.

Interacting with your bird and trying to gain his trust will also go a long way in helping him overcome his phobia and become more confident.

Jealousy
Parrots can become jealous of new people in your family very easily. For instance, if you get married, the parrot may become jealous of your spouse. The real issue is when the jealousy is targeted towards a newborn.

Show the bird that having the person he is jealous of in the same room means that he has some advantages. This could be a gentle rub on the head or even a treat. Normally, when we have a newborn in the house, especially, we tend to ignore the bird in the presence of the baby. So, the bird quickly associates the child with neglect. You do not have to let the bird out of the cage, of course. With the baby or any other person that the jealously is targeted at in the same room, have some interaction with your bird.

Encourage the other person to build a relationship with the bird. This can mean giving the bird a treat occasionally and eventually encouraging the bird to step up on the person's hand or finger. The more the bird trusts the other person, the less he will be jealous.

This is not something you can accomplish in a day or even a few days. It will take time for your bird to trust another person completely.

All you need to be aware of is the information that you are passing on to the bird. If you are away from your bird every time that person is around, jealousy will build. Instead, both of you can try and interact with the bird and shower him with the attention he wants.

Feather plucking
If your bird suddenly begins to pluck his own feathers out in an agitated manner or over-preens himself to the extent that he mutilates his skin and feathers, then it means that he has developed the issue of feather plucking.

When your bird resorts to feather plucking, you will see several bald spots. In addition to that, you will find feathers on the floor of the cage even when it is not molting season.

There are several reasons for feather plucking in Ringnecks, including:

- **Malnutrition:** If the diet of the bird is deprived of minerals like zinc, calcium, selenium and manganese, the skin becomes irritable, leading to feather plucking.

- **Boredom:** When the cage is too small for the bird to move around or if he does not have enough activities to keep him mentally stimulated, feather plucking becomes a means to keep himself engaged.

- **Lack of natural light:** Sunlight is a source of vitamin D. If your bird is kept in a dark area for long hours, he will become very depressed. This manifests in the form of feather plucking.

- **Stress:** If your bird is unwell or if he is in an environment that makes him feel stressed, such as a pet lurking around the cage very often, then feather plucking will begin. There are some medicines and supplements that can help him overcome feather plucking associated with stress. Treating the primary health issue will also reduce feather plucking in your bird.

- **Loneliness:** Ringnecks are solitary birds in the wild. However, it does not mean that they do not need any companionship. Spending time with your bird or finding him a compatible cage mate can help solve feather plucking related to loneliness.

- **Pain:** With birds, pain is not a feeling that they are able to understand. They know that they are uncomfortable and will try to relieve themselves by plucking feathers off the area where the pain is concentrated. There are also health issues like Psittacosis and Aspergillosis that have been commonly associated with feather plucking in birds. Your bird may have ingested a foreign object that makes his crop irritable, leading to this behavioral issue.

- **Food allergies:** Sensitivity towards a certain type of food will lead to feather plucking. Changing the diet or the brand of food that you give your bird is an effective way to deal with feather plucking.

In addition to the above, hormonal imbalance, improper diet and toxicosis can also lead to feather plucking in birds. Since there are so many causes for this condition, it is best that you let your vet examine the bird first before you begin to treat your bird.

Once the primary causal factor is eliminated, there are several medicines that will help the feathers grow back. You can also spray the body with an aloe vera solution to make the skin less irritable and promote the growth of feathers.

4. Common injuries

Birds are prone to injuries from time to time. Making sure that the bird gets immediate first aid is the best way to prevent the condition from getting worse. Before that, you will have to recognize the symptoms of common injuries and accidents to provide the correct assistance to your Ringneck.

Broken blood feather
- When you are clipping the wings of the bird, sometimes, you can get a blood feather, which will lead to profuse bleeding.

- The best way to deal with this is to remove the broken feather entirely. If you are not sure about how to do this, take your bird to the vet.

- First, you need to stop the bleeding. This can be done by applying some flour on the area or by running a styptic pencil on the injured area.

Constricted toes
- This is a very common condition in baby birds. This occurs when the humidity in the brooding or nesting box is low.

- The toes of the bird will seem scaly and will lead to a lot of irritation.

- If the condition progresses, blood flow to the affected toe will be cut off and the toe can become dry and will eventually fall off.

- Consult your vet to get a skin cream that can soften the skin. When it is soft enough, the scaly skin can be peeled off carefully.

Crop burn
- This is yet another common condition in baby birds. Luckily, it can be resolved quite easily.

- If the crop feathers have not developed yet, the bird is more susceptible to this condition.

- A blister or a patch of white skin is seen on the crop. This is caused by a burn on the crop.

- Make sure that the food that you give your baby bird is the right temperature to prevent crop burn.

- Stir your finger in the food to make sure that there are no hot spots in it.

- If you notice a blister, make sure you call your vet immediately. When left unattended, this condition can be fatal to baby birds.

Dehydration
- This is a condition that can affect your Ringneck at any age. You will notice that the skin is red and is very elastic.

- If you pick the skin slightly, it will stay wrinkled when the bird is dehydrated.

- In baby birds, dehydration can be caused by a bacterial infection that makes digestion slow.

- The first thing that you should do is to rehydrate the bird immediately. The vet can give your bird a Ringers' solution injection to help him recover immediately.

- Adding some apple juice or a fruit that your bird enjoys in the water can urge him to consume water.

- You can even give the bird Pedialyte to restore the water level in the body immediately.

- Make sure that clean and fresh water is available to your bird at all times. Birds will not consume water that may have some fecal matter or debris in it.

Broken wings
- Running into walls, getting caught in ropes used to suspend toys or even a fight can lead to broken wings in birds.

- You will see that the wing hangs down from the side of the body and that the bird is hesitant to move and will resort to a corner on the floor of the cage.

- The first thing to do is to move the cage to an area that is free from any stress.

- If the bird is not hand trained, pick him up by wrapping a towel around him.

- Hold the feather in place and tape it in place with gauze. Using surgical tape or sticky tape can damage the feathers.

- Then, rush him to the vet immediately.

Split sternum
- A split sternum occurs when the breastbone breaks and punctures the skin on the chest of the bird.

- This is caused when the bird falls on a hard surface or when he is attacked by another bird or a pet.

- Birds that have clipped wings are prone to this accident.

- The skin on the chest must be sutured and therefore you must take the bird to the vet immediately.

- This injury should be prevented by ensuring that the cage is not placed on a hard surface or near one.

Cuts and wounds
- If you see a scrape or wound on the body of the bird, it must be cleaned with an antiseptic solution immediately.

- For a mild cut, you can apply some styptic powder to clot the blood and then apply an antiseptic cream or rinse with hydrogen peroxide.

- If the wound is deep, hold a piece of gauze on it and apply some pressure. This will control the bleeding while the bird is taken to the vet.

Burns
- Landing on a hot stove or grazing against a hot bulb while flying can lead to burns.

- The burnt area should be held under cold running water to ease to pain.

- If it is a mild burn you can apply burn cream or antiseptic on the area and allow it to heal.

- In case of severe burns, your bird will need immediate veterinary attention.

Sour crop
- This is a condition that occurs only in baby birds that are being hand fed.

- It is important for the crop to be emptied entirely at least once a day.

- If this does not happen, the food in the crop will begin to spoil and will slow down digestion.

- Inserting a feeding tube to clean the crop is one way to empty it.

- You can also hold the bird upside down and then massage the crop area to push the food out of the mouth. This is risky, as it can lead to food getting into the respiratory system if your bird panics.

- If you do not know how to insert the feeding tube, do not attempt to do it, as it can rupture the esophagus. Make sure that you consult someone with more experience.

With these common injuries, prevention is definitely better than cure. Make sure that the environment of the bird is safe and that you follow the right techniques of feeding and grooming your bird to prevent accidents.

5. First aid kit for birds
Having a first aid kit is very important to make sure that your bird gets immediate attention when he has an injury or an accident. You must keep a kit with the following items handy at all times:

- Styptic pencil or powder
- Medicated gauze
- Cotton pads
- A small syringe to clean wounds or provide medicines
- Ink dropper
- Tweezers
- A pair of small scissors
- Antiseptic cream recommended by the vet
- Hydrogen peroxide to wash wounds and burns
- Sterile saline solution
- A pair of gloves
- A towel to handle the bird easily
- The number of your vet
- Poison control numbers
- Cotton ear buds to apply ointments and medicines

Alternatively, you can also purchase commercially prepared first aid kits that will be easily available at your vet. Some are also available online. Make sure that you find one that is recommended by your vet to be sure that it contains everything that you will need in case of an emergency.

When your bird is with a pet sitter or is being taken care of by a friend or relative, make sure that you provide them with all the emergency contact details to take care of a sudden medical emergency.

The last and most important thing is to contact your insurance company to find out about options for your Ringneck. There are some insurance companies that your vet will also be able to recommend to cover for any major surgery, unexpected medical needs or even for third party damage caused by your bird.

If you are not able to find a satisfactory insurance policy, you must set aside medical emergency funds for your bird to be prepared for an untoward situation.

Conclusion

This book has, hopefully, prepared you for your feathered friend. The purpose of this book is to make sure that you are ready to take on the responsibility of an Indian Ringneck.

As you have read already, it is a lot of work and can be physically, emotionally and financially taxing for the owner to take good care of the bird. However, the companionship that you get for a lifetime is absolutely worth it.

Thank you for choosing this book. The efforts in providing you with genuine and practical information are sincere. Hopefully, that will translate into a good relationship with your beloved parrot.

Make sure that you take your role as a parrot owner seriously. These exquisite birds are a wonder of nature with their amazing cognitive abilities and their perfect temperament to fit into any home that is willing to make the effort.

The more time you devote to your bird, the more you will understand what he needs to be happy. That way you will be able to amass all the right information to keep your Indian Ringneck healthy all through his life and enjoy your journey with him.

References

The information with respect to Indian Ringnecks available out there is endless. It can become confusing for you to find information that is genuine and reliable. Here are a few options that you can use as a reference whenever you need a little more assistance to raise your Indian Ringneck. Remember, the more you learn, the easier it will become to handle your bird.

Note: at the time of printing, all the websites below were working. As the internet changes rapidly, some sites might no longer be live when you read this book. That is, of course, out of our control.

www.indianRingneck.com

www.animalplanet85.blogspot.in

www.parrotsecrets.com

www.beautyofbirds.com

www.naturechest.com

www.birdsville.net.au

www.kijiji.ca

www.parrotsecrets.com

www.thespruce.com

www.parrotsdailynews.com

www.animals.mom.me

www.pets.thenest.com

www.sciencedirect.com

www.informationvine.com

www.peteducation.com

www.quora.com

www.parrotsnaturally.com

www.parrotscanada.com

www.adoptapet.com

www.companionparrots.org

www.linkinghub.elsevier.com

www.pets.thenest.com

www.astepupbird.com/

www.longtailedparakeets.blogspot.com

www.northernparrots.com

www.windycityparrot.com

www.pbspettravel.co.uk

www.Ringneckranch.net

www.riveroflifefarm.com

Lightning Source UK Ltd.
Milton Keynes UK
UKHW010845260419

341665UK00010B/911/P